HOUSTON IS COOKING
The Best

by Ann Criswell

Nutritionist
Linda McDonald, M.S., R.D., L.D.

Wine Consultant
Denman Moody

Editorial Assistant
Ann Steiner

Foreword
Bob Lanier
Mayor of Houston

Tribute
Richard J. V. Johnson
Chairman and Publisher
The Houston Chronicle

 **Publisher**
Fran Fauntleroy

HOUSTON IS COOKING
The Best

OUR SPECIAL THANKS TO

Ed Daniels - *Photography*

Mark Ruisinger - *Galloway Florist - Flowers*

B & C Partners - *Graphic Design*

Nancy Hudgins - *Publicity*

Wetmore & Company - *Printing*

Events - *Table Appointments; China: Versace*

Spec's Liquor Store - *John Rydman*

Tarrant Distributors, Inc.

Rice Epicurean Markets

Houston Chronicle - *Betty Tichich: Ann Criswell's Photo*

Special Friends

Houston Gourmet
Houston, Texas

Copyright ©1996 by Houston Gourmet

Printed in the United States of America

ISBN 1-882296-03-6

Library of Congress Cataloging-In-Publication data
Houston Gourmet Publishing Company

All recipes are reprinted with permission of authors.
Photographs printed with permission of Ed Daniels.
LiteFare and nutritional information printed with permission of Linda McDonald.

FOREWORD BY BOB LANIER

MAYOR OF HOUSTON

Elyse and I have always called the Houston area home and for years we have enjoyed all that Houston's restaurants and chefs have to offer. I'm pleased to have been given the opportunity to write the foreword for this wonderful book.

Houston has grown and changed over the past decades - from a small city centered around the oil business to a booming, sophisticated metroplex with a diverse community and economy. And Houston's restaurants reflect the wonderful diversity of our citizens.

I strongly believe Houston's diversity is our greatest asset. Houston is positioned to take this country's lead as we move toward a global economy because Houstonians recognize that our differences make us strong. Just a quick glance at the recipes in this book is proof that making the most of different cultures can only serve to make our lives richer.

In the mood for Asian food? Drive to Houston's southwest neighborhoods where you have your pick of authentic and delicious

Asian restaurants. Or try midtown, where a myriad of Vietnamese restaurants play host to business people, theater crowds and families.

Looking for Mexican food? Our strong Hispanic ties give way to so many excellent restaurants. Inside or outside the Loop, diners can choose from Middle Eastern, Italian, German and American cafes that have brought Houston some much deserved recognition. New Orleans, New York, San Francisco - now Houston is part of that elite group of cities known for fine dining. Visitors and Houstonians alike should be proud of the fine service, excellent food and the wide range of choices our restaurants offer. We're home to an amazing collection of chefs, and the camaraderie among them is one more reason "Houston Is Cooking The Best".

As our economy grows and our inner city neighborhoods continue to thrive, so do the small bistros that in recent years have sprouted up near downtown. They offer citizens one more reason to come downtown. I urge you to take a "vacation." Spend a weekend treating Houston as if you were a tourist. Spend time in one of our beautiful parks, take in a show downtown, stop by a street festival and treat yourself to one of our many fine restaurants. I guarantee it will be time well spent!

Enjoy!

Bob Lanier
Mayor of Houston

"Just a quick glance at the recipes in this book is proof that making the most of different cultures can only serve to make our lives richer."

A FIVE-STAR TRIBUTE TO ANN CRISWELL ★★★★★

Picture if you will, a girl in the little East Texas town of Mineola. A girl who loves black-eyed peas, cornbread, fried chicken and rice and gravy, and who will come to be recognized as Houston's foremost authority on cooking.

That could only have been Ann Criswell, who for thirty years has been the Chronicle's food editor and who — I am delighted to say — chose the Chronicle long before we chose her. After graduating from Texas Woman's University in Denton, where she came to know Mrs. John T. Jones, wife of the late Chronicle president, Ann was determined to work for the paper.

She was so determined that she interviewed for jobs in several departments, even classified advertising but there were no openings at the time.

Then, in April 1961, one of her dreams came true and another had its beginning. Ann joined the Chronicle as home furnishings editor. In 1962, she was named society editor. After years of writing about debutantes and the social whirl, she returned to home furnishings until she was named food editor and the Criswell dream began. She not only created the paper's first food section, for about 10 years she wrote and edited almost every word and supervised production of a 20- to 30- page section each week.

Hers has been the exciting story of watching, nurturing and reporting the story of cooking in Houston. In the '60s there were only four or five restaurants in town that rated "good." There were Madeline's, Ye Old College Inn, Sonny Look's and Maxim's.

It all begin to change, Ann says, in the '70s when Houstonians began to travel abroad. They came home hungry for something other than the traditional dishes of the South. That is when, for the first time, she believes, gourmet cooking came to Houston.

What Ann doesn't say, but is true, is that she had the perception to recognize what was happening. It was she, more than any other chef or domestic cook, who led Houston to be acknowledged today as the "undiscovered dining-out city in America."

And again, it was Ann Criswell who saw and encouraged the impact of Houston's diverse ethnic community that today satisfies our taste buds with dishes from countries all over the world.

You have made Houston a city that knows what bon appetit means, Ann. You are very special to the Chronicle and to Houston and we all love you.

Richard J.V. Johnson
Chairman and Publisher
The Houston Chronicle

INTRODUCTION

ANN CRISWELL
Food Editor
The Houston Chronicle

When I became editor of the first Food Section at the Houston Chronicle 30 years ago, Houston dined on beef and bourbon (carried into restaurants in brown paper bags when permitted) and most restaurant patrons expected little more than steak, fried chicken and barbecue. Since then, chefs and restaurants have given us a taste for the new and exciting from tropical fruits and newly cultivated vegetables to wild game, fish and better (and more healthful) beef. Particularly in the past 10 years, restaurants have become a major influence on the local food scene.

Their unique dishes cross various geographical and cultural lines mirroring Houston's growth as a global city. They have increased our appreciation of the fine dining experience from cooking techniques to plate presentation.

Recent trends include the resurgence of steakhouses and the opening of seafood restaurants, American grills and microbreweries as well as casual Italian, African, Middle Eastern, Persian, Japanese, Thai, Vietnamese and other Asian, vegetarian and South American restaurants.

Almost 1,000 restaurants opened in Houston in 1995, and it is predicted that Houston consumers will spend almost $4 billion eating out in 1996.

What Houstonians have enjoyed when dining out, they often wish to recreate at home, and "Houston Is Cooking The Best" is our seventh cookbook to fill that need. Twenty-six of the city's best chefs and restaurants share their recipes for popular dishes that are sure to become home favorites, too.

They also share many of their cooking secrets and ideas for versatile ingredients such as roasted tomatoes, corn, garlic and chilies.

Through their recipes, you will discover that many Caribbean, Thai- and Creole-style sauces or fruits, smoked chilies and salsas compliment American beef, chicken and vegetables as well as they do authentic ethnic dishes.

To broaden your cooking horizons with the recipes in this book, you will need extra-virgin olive oil; flavored oils and vinegars; ancho, chipotle, poblano, serrano and other fresh and dried chilies; high-quality fresh and dried pasta; shallots; mustards; lemon and lime zest; Roma tomatoes (the deep red, teardrop-shaped Italian tomatoes), black beans; exotic mushrooms such as portobello, shiitake, oyster and porcini; cotija, mascarpone and goat cheese; ginger; cilantro; and field greens, various combinations of gourmet baby lettuces and greens.

The quality and integrity of the ingredients are significant to the success of many dishes, so make substitutions thoughtfully. In the Special Helps section at the back of this book we've included cooking terms and descriptions of techniques used by professional chefs — clarifying butter, making brown stock and roux, deglazing a pan and basic techniques for roasting chilies, garlic, peppers and other vegetables.

We hope "Houston Is Cooking The Best" will challenge you to experiment and inspire you to get together with friends for cooking parties. It's also fun to work your way through the book with a series of restaurant-hopping parties. Take advantage of the exciting food Houston has to offer in or out of the kitchen.

TABLE OF CONTENTS

FOREWORD 5

TRIBUTE 7

INTRODUCTION 8

ABOUT ANN CRISWELL 12

DINING WITH WINE 13

AMERICAS AND CHURRASCOS 15
Pargo Americas
Torta de Queso y Maiz
Caramanolas
Cerdo a la Puchica

ANTHONY'S AND LA GRIGLIA 19
Anthony's Seared Shrimp with Spicy Mango Salsa
Blackberry Crustade
Snapper La Griglia
Joey's Nutty Salad

BRENNAN'S AND THIRD COAST 23
Texas Creole Barbecue Shrimp with Jicama Salad
and Texas Cornbread Pudding
Chocolate Peanut Butter Fudge Pie
Mama's Carrot Cake
Third Coast Crabcakes with Lemon Butter Sauce
& Pico de Gallo

THE BROWNSTONE 27
Sweet Potato-Chipotle Bisque
Grilled Caribbean Shrimp with Cuban Barbecue Sauce
and Orange-Jalapeno Risotto
Grilled Quail and Portobello Mushroom Salad

CAFE CASPIAN 33
Yogurt and Spinach Dip
Chicken Kabab
Rice with Lima Beans

CAVATORE 37
Insalata del Cuoco
Marinara Sauce
Rigatoni alla Verdure
Scallopini di Pollo

CHEZ NOUS 41
Chilled Leek Soup
Saute of Chanterelle Mushrooms with Corn
Steamed Striped Bass with Wilted Spinach,
Sweet Pepper and Lime Sauce
Figs and Berries with Key Lime Sorbet and Sabayon

DAMIAN'S 45
Shrimp Damian
Pollo Menichino
Fedilini Buongustaio
Lamb Chops Arno

DECO AT THE ADAM'S MARK HOTEL 49
Pan Seared Pork Tenderloin with Macadamia Nut
Chutney and Granny Smith Vinaigrette
Cornflake Cinnamon Raisin Toast
Bread Pudding with Kentucky Bourbon Whiskey Sauce

DEVILLE AT THE FOUR SEASONS 55
Carpaccio of Beefsteak Tomatoes with Spinach,
Arugula and Balsamic Vinaigrette
Penne Pasta with Sauteed Chicken
and Spinach Cream Sauce
Grilled Beef Tenderloin on Potato-Thyme Cake
with Chipotle Cream
Pumpkin Cream Brule with Fresh Berry Compote

EMPRESS 59
Boneless Quail with Shredded Vegetables Flambe
Crispy Chicken with Lemon Sauce
Peanuts and Ginger Soup
Chocolate Brownie Fudge

TABLE OF CONTENTS

THE HOUSTONIAN 63
Grilled Corn Soup with Avocado Pico de Gallo
Yakitori Salmon Salad with Buckwheat Noodles
    and Ponzu Dressing
Mango Rice Pudding with Ginger Candy Crust

LA TOUR D'ARGENT 67
Gazpacho El Rey
Smoked Salmon Julienne with Endive
Roast Lamb Rack with Herb and Mustard
Grand Marnier Souffle

MOOSE CAFE 71
Smoked Tomato and Spinach Dip
Salmon Cakes
Spinach Quesadillas
Lemon Chess Pie

POST OAK GRILL AND REDWOOD GRILL 77
Ancho Chili Soup
Balsamic Angel Hair Pasta with Chicken
Nantucket Bleu Spinach Salad
Amaretto Cheesecake with Amaretto Glaze and
    Chocolate Sauce

RANCHO TEJAS 81
Stuffed Jalapenos Chihuahuas
Grilled Stuffed Flounder with Crabmeat Shrimp Stuffing
    and Tejas Pecan Butter
Frijoles a las Charras Poblanos
Pecan Cobbler

RIVIERA GRILL 85
Grilled Shrimp with Roasted Red Pepper Risotto
Pepper-Crusted Sea Bass with Kalamata Olives, Garlic,
    Capers and Tomato Ragout
Caponata
Grilled Center-Cut Pork Chops with
    Scotch Bonnet Fruit Chutney
Warm Bittersweet Chocolate Torte

RIVOLI 89
Acorn Squash Soup
Stuffed Dover Sole
Tournedos Voronoff
Blanc Mange Romanoff

ROTISSERIE FOR BEEF AND BIRD 93
Smoked Chicken Salad with Papaya Salsa
Medallions of Venison with Chile-Pepper Sauce
Praline Ice Cream Parfait with Caramelized Pecans
    and Chocolate Sauce

TONY'S AND GROTTO 99
Roasted Peppers with Fontina
Osso Buco with Balsamic Vinegar and
    Risotto alla Milanese
Penne Pasta with Arugula
Chicken Positano with Italian Spinach

VIVA! 103
Black Beans
Black Bean Burrito
Ranchero Sauce
Viva! Pasta
Spinach Enchiladas
Peach Melba Smoothie

ABOUT LINDA MCDONALD 107

HEALTHY RECIPE MODIFICATIONS 108

SPECIAL HELPS 110

SHOPPING GUIDE 112

NUTRITIONAL ANALYSIS 116

INDEX 120

BIOGRAPHIES 123

WHO'S WHO 124
(Key to Back Cover Photograph)

ORDER FORM

ABOUT ANN CRISWELL

Ann Criswell has been employed at the Houston Chronicle for 35 years and has been food editor since 1966. She has written freelance food articles, authored seven cookbooks and edited several others. As food editor of the Chronicle she contributed most of the recipes in the "Texas the Beautiful Cookbook" published in October 1986.

She is a member of the Association of Food Journalists, Houston Culinary Guild and Houston Culinary Historians.

In 1987, she was named the first honorary member of the South Texas Dietetic Association and received an award of excellence from the American Heart Association, American Cancer Society and Texas Restaurant Association. In 1992, she was named Media Person of the Year by the Texas Dietetic Association.

Because of a special interest in wine, she wrote a wine column for many years and has made several wine tours in Europe and California. She also has judged Texas wine competitions and national cooking contests including the National Beef Cook-Off and Pillsbury Bake-Off. In 1993, she was chief judge for the National Chicken Cooking Contest.

She is an honor graduate of Texas Woman's University. Her late husband, Jim, was a Houston newspaperman. She has a daughter, Catherine; son, Charles; and four grandchildren, Ryan and Christopher Criswell and James and Ann Claire Lester.

DINING WITH WINE BY DENMAN MOODY

A complementary wine can make a good food dish great, and vice-versa. A Chateau Latour 1961 - one of the world's greatest red wines - served with a chocolate sundae would do irreparable harm to each.

In attempting to pair some old and brand new wine names with these fabulous dishes so as to create a culinary synergism, I have sought the counsel of my friends Lindy and John Rydman at Spec's, and Jim DeGeorge and Lenoir Josey, my two best wine-drinking buddies over the last 20 years, all having vast wine knowledge and many years of trial and error experimenting with wine-food match-ups. A special thanks is extended to Tarrant Distributors and their bon vivant leader, Neil Strauss, and to Barry Johnson of Grand Crew Importers. Book learning in this game pales by comparison to the empirical method.

For each recipe I have listed the least expensive wine first, followed by two others in ascending price scale. Most of the first wines listed will be under $10. The middle wine will normally be in the $10-$20 range and the third wine will be, in most instances, around $20 or more. If there is a fourth wine, it will be the "ne plus ultra" wine for that course with price no object.

Many of these wines are from other countries and will be so noted. Sherries, Ports and Madeiras will be mentioned without reference to origin. A wine with no country or state noted will be from California.

Although vintages are not listed for each wine, it is very important to note that in Bordeaux, '85, '86, '88, '89 and '90 are all very good to astounding. So if you are doing any cellaring, these vintages are a must for purchasing now, to the extent available.

For red Burgundy, '88 and '90 and to some degree '89 and '93 are the best wines to buy and cellar or drink now.

California North Coast cabernets are a different story: '88 and '89 were not as good as '85, '86, '87, '90, '91, '92, '93 and '94. It's hard to go too far off base with a good quality North Coast cabernet from '90 to the present.

In Tuscany, '88 and '90 are the great vintages, and in Piedmont, '88, '89 and '90 are the biggies. But they're disappearing fast.

For white Burgundies and California and Australian chardonnays, the vintage is just not as important as it is for the reds, in my opinion.

The optimum way to receive a benefit from this book would be as follows: Each of three couples prepare one recipe - an appetizer, entree or dessert - and each bring one or two of the wines recommended here. Discuss how the recipe could be improved (if possible) and which wines might be as good or even better with the dish!

All of us hope that you will enjoy this book; share it with your friends.

p.s. It will make a great Christmas, birthday or anniversary present and will benefit all of us, starting with myself, by raising wine and food appreciation to a new level of enjoyment in our community.

DENMAN MOODY

Denman Moody, connoisseur and wine writer, was editor and publisher of "Moody's Wine Review," which the "Washington Post" said was the "...best publication in this country for tracking the state of rare and exotic wines."

Denman is a former Host of the Houston Chapter of the International Wine and Food Society, as well as Commander Emeritus of the Knights of the Vine. He is also Vice President of Amici della Vite and a member of the Commanderie de Bordeaux.

His wine articles have appeared in numerous publications including: "Revue du Vin de France," Paris; "International Wine and Food Society Journal," London; "International Wine Review;" "Wine and Spirits" and "Texas Monthly."

In his spare time, Denman is a financial consultant.

PARGO AMERICAS
TORTA DE QUESO Y MAIZ
CARAMANOLAS
CERDO A LA PUCHICA

Americas awes guests first with its multi-level architecture then with its trail-blazing cuisine. The owners are from Nicaragua and the menu introduces us to the indigenous foods of North, Central, Latin and South America — corn, potatoes, tomatoes, peanuts, chocolate and chilies. Co-owner/chef Michael Cordua says he interchanges the basic ingredients of the various American cuisines to achieve new tastes.

Swashbuckling design by Chicago architect Jordan Mozer creates somewhat surreal, but high-energy surroundings; a 45-foot high "woven wall," suspended stairway of steel and slate, black mosaic tile tree trunks and handmade fixtures hark back to fabled pre-Columbian times, the mountains of Machu Picchu and the colors, natural elements, rope bridges and artifacts of the ancient Incas.

Only four months after it opened, Americas was cited as the best new restaurant in America in 1993 by Esquire restaurant critic John Mariani. Cordua, named one of the Ten Best New Chefs in America by Food & Wine magazine in 1994, also was one of 13 chefs to receive the Robert Mondavi Award for Culinary Excellence. His brother and co-owner, Glenn Cordua, assembled the award-winning wine list to compliment such signature dishes as Pargo Americas, corn-crusted snapper with shrimp accompanied by sauteed corn in corn husk boats; and various seafood, lamb, pork, black bean and yuca (cassava) dishes.

Americas and Churrascos also are famous for desserts including Tres Leches (Three Milk) Cake and Torta de Queso y Maiz (an unusual cheesecake made with cream cheese and creamed corn).

Churrascos is named for a South American specialty, a charcoal-grilled steak (usually a tougher cut) butterflied in a unique jellyroll fashion. Here the meat is upgraded to center-cut prime beef tenderloin basted with chimichurri sauce, the South American equivalent of pesto.

The Cordua brothers own two Churrascos restaurants; the original was named one of America's best new restaurants in 1989. The menu focuses on South American dishes including empanadas, black bean soup, char-grilled meats, arepas (corn cakes), shrimp and fresh tuna. The sauces used in many of the restaurant dishes — chimichurri, Mireya and Amazon — and the plantain chips are now being marketed as Cordua's Flavors from the Rainforest products in specialty supermarkets.

Americas
1800 Post Oak Blvd.
Houston, Tx 77056
961-1492

Churrascos
2055 Westheimer
Houston, Tx 77098
527-8300

Churrascos
9705 Westheimer
Houston, Tx 77042
952-1988

——————— *LITE FARE* ———————

South American cuisine features trimmed lean meats, seafood, black beans, fresh vegetables and fruits; all good choices for the healthy diner. Request that dishes be prepared dry (without added fat) and sauces served on the side. Chimichurri is a type of pesto used on grilled items. A variety of grilled and steamed vegetables are available.

PARGO AMERICAS

3	ears white corn, divided
3	tablespoons oil, divided
1	garlic clove, minced
2	each, finely diced: red and green jalapenos
3	tablespoons chopped fresh cilantro
1/2	pound shrimp, peeled and deveined, for garnish Achiote powder (see Special Helps section) Salt and freshly ground black pepper to taste
4	(6-ounce) red snapper fillets Flour for dredging
4	egg whites, beaten Crema Fresca (Mexican sour cream, available at Fiesta)

Preheat oven to 350 degrees. Shuck corn and save four husks to create "boats" to hold sauteed corn. Cut kernels from cobs. Place half of kernels on a baking sheet. Bake 15 to 20 minutes, until crisp and light brown in color. Let cool; reserve.

Heat 1 tablespoon oil in skillet; sauté remaining corn in oil with garlic and jalapenos. Sprinkle with cilantro and place in corn husk boats. Sprinkle shrimp with achiote and marinate about 1 hour; then, sauté until just firm. Salt and pepper fillets; lightly dredge in flour on both sides. Shake off excess; dip in egg whites. Press fillets firmly onto roasted and cooled corn.

Heat remaining 2 tablespoons oil in large skillet over medium-high heat. Sauté fillets 4 to 5 minutes on one side; turn over, sauté 3 to 4 minutes on other side. Line each plate with Crema Fresca and place fillet on top of sauce. Place one shrimp in each corn husk to garnish each plate.

Serves 4.

Use 1 cup Crema Fresca. Substitute fat-free sour cream for the Crema Fresca.

Fall Creek or Llano Estacado Chenin Blanc (Texas); Chappallet Chenin Blanc; Chateau Moncontour Vouvray (France).

TORTA DE QUESO Y MAIZ

This intriguing cheesecake containing creamed corn is a signature dessert at Americas. At the restaurant, the cheesecake is garnished with a sprinkling of Cracker Jacks.

4	(8-ounce) packages cream cheese, softened
1/2	cup (1 stick) butter
2	cups sour cream
1 1/2	cups sugar
7	tablespoons cornstarch
1	tablespoon vanilla
2	cups canned creamed corn
2	tablespoons fresh lemon juice
5	eggs

Preheat oven to 375 degrees. Butter and flour a 10-inch springform pan; set aside. In an electric mixer, combine cream cheese and butter; beat until creamy. Blend in sour cream, sugar, cornstarch, vanilla, corn and lemon juice. Add eggs, one at a time, beating well after each addition. Pour batter into prepared pan and bake 1 hour. Turn off oven and leave cheesecake inside another hour with door closed. Remove from oven and cool 2 hours; refrigerate until well chilled.

Serves 16.

Substitute light sour cream and cream cheese for regular.

Bargetto Olallieberry Wine; KWV Ruby Port (South Africa); Quady Essensia.

CARAMANOLAS

1	cup cooked black beans
1/4	cup olive oil
1	cup minced onion, divided
1/4	cup (1/2 stick) butter
1	tablespoon each: Worcestershire and bottled red pepper sauces
1	pound chorizo
1	cup ground cotija cheese (Mexican farmer's cheese)
2	tablespoons finely chopped fresh green jalapenos
1	pound yuca, peeled Oil for deep frying Red Pepper Sauce (recipe follows)

Drain black beans; puree. Heat 1/4 cup oil in a skillet; fry 1/2 cup onion until very dark, almost burned. Discard onion. Add beans, butter, Worcestershire and bottled red pepper sauce to skillet; fry until mixture is cooked dry enough to flip in pan like an omelet, about 30 minutes.

Remove chorizo from casing, crumble into a skillet and cook until browned; drain on paper towels. Add chorizo, cheese, remaining 1/2 cup onion and jalapenos to black bean mixture. Mix and allow to cool.

Boil yuca in salted water until tender, about 20 minutes. Drain, remove center root and mash. Form 12 balls; flatten each into a 5-inch round. Place 2 tablespoons black bean filling in center. Fold in half and seal edges.

Preheat oil in deep fryer to 375 degrees. Fry Caramanolas in batches until golden brown, about 5 minutes.

To serve: Coat plate with Cordua brand Amazon Dressing (available at local grocery stores, Churrascos and Americas restaurants). Using a squirt bottle, draw concentric circles of Red Pepper Sauce on top of Amazon Dressing. From center, use a knife to "pull" red sauce towards edge of plate. Place two Caramanolas on top of sauce.

RED PEPPER SAUCE

8	ounces chipotle chilies (dried, smoked jalapenos)
1/4	cup water

Red Pepper Sauce
Puree chilies and water in blender.

Serves 6.

 Cherish just one.

 Margarita or Mexican beer.

CERDO A LA PUCHICA

4 pork tenderloins (about
3 pounds)
Salt and freshly ground black
pepper to taste
2 cups all-purpose flour
1/2 cup olive oil, divided
1 cup chopped red bell pepper,
divided
Lemon Butter Sauce (recipe
follows), divided
1 cup chopped green onion,
divided

Remove any silver skin from pork. Cut each tenderloin in half to make two (6-inch) portions. Turn meat so that one cut side is parallel to cutting board. With a sharp knife, cut straight down at one side and moving knife continuously to the right unroll tenderloin until it is a thin, rectangular portion. This is the method used for Churrascos' and Americas' signature "churrascos" steaks. Repeat process with each piece (see note). Place meat between two sheets of plastic and pound until evenly flat. Cut each in half. Repeat process with each tenderloin.

Salt and pepper pork, dust lightly with flour. Heat 2 tablespoons oil in a large skillet and add 2 pieces of pork, smooth side down. Sauté pork on one side until golden brown. Turn, add 2 tablespoons bell pepper and cook 1 minute. Remove from heat and add 2 tablespoons Lemon Butter Sauce and 2 tablespoons chopped green onion. Remove pork and sauce from skillet; keep warm until ready to use. Repeat procedure with remaining pork.

Note: An alternative method is to cut the pork into 1-inch thick medallions and pound them flat with a mallet between sheets of plastic wrap.

LEMON BUTTER SAUCE

1/4 cup demi-glace (can be store-
bought) or beef stock (see
Special Helps section)
Juice of 1 each: lime and lemon
1 pound (4 sticks) butter at room
temperature
1 teaspoon each: salt and white
pepper

Lemon Butter Sauce

Heat demi-glace and juices in a skillet over medium-high heat until bubbling. Reduce heat so that sauce just simmers. Slowly whisk in butter, about 4 tablespoons at a time, until all is incorporated. Add salt and pepper; keep warm over a pan of simmering water until ready to use. Makes about 2 cups; reserve extra for another use.

Serves 8.

🍎 Eliminate oil by sauteing pork tenderloins in a nonstick skillet using nonstick spray. Use just 1/2 cup Lemon Butter Sauce which is 1 tablespoon per serving.

🍇 White: Trefethen White Riesling; Santa Margherita Pinot Grigio (Italy); Byron Chardonnay.
Red: Sebastiani Heritage Zinfandel; Ridge Petite Syrah; Kline Mourvedre Reserve.

ANTHONY'S SEARED SHRIMP
with Spicy Mango Salsa
BLACKBERRY CRUSTADE
SNAPPER LA GRIGLIA
JOEY'S NUTTY SALAD

At Anthony's, the glass-enclosed kitchen with wood-burning rotisserie and hearth sets the stage for refined bistro food with French, Italian and American influences. The restaurant moved to Highland Village in 1994. An attention-getting burgundy red exterior opens to reveal a polished hardwood entry, mahogany bar and a chic, but cozy, ambiance with touches of hunter green, brass and lead glass. A Renaissance bas relief by Rusty Arena covers one long wall of the dining room.

Anthony's is one of Houston's designated meeting places for business luncheons, dining with friends and celebrating romantic and special occasions. The Wine Library, accommodates small gatherings in a semiprivate setting.

ANTHONY'S

Bruce McMillian, chef at Anthony's for eight years, has created a sophisticated menu of seafood, fish, duck and pasta specials, substantial salads and grilled dishes, which changes seasonally. Specialties include Avocado Pancakes (with crab claws, lump crab and salsa); Lobster Souffle; Ermy Salad (sliced fennel, feta, cured olives, tomatoes and greens); Osso Buco with risotto; and a tempting array of signature desserts such as Key Lime Pie and Cup of Cappuccino, a velvety cross between pot de creme and mocha mousse. A fixed-price, three-course business luncheon is a popular recent addition.

la griglia

La Griglia, which opened in 1991, is a restaurant for the '90s. The menu melds traditional Italian and contemporary cooking in a colorful, energy-charged, high-tech setting favored by up-and-coming professionals. Colorful mosaic columns and wall murals by Jan Parsons define dining areas.

Chef Genaro Carmano supervises the kitchen and prepares rotisserie and open-hearth specialties, pasta dishes, interesting salads, seafood, fish and veal dishes. La Griglia's roasted garlic, which is simmered in milk before roasting, is particularly noteworthy.

A three-course business luncheon and spa selections, which are low in sodium, fat and calories, appeal to today's health-conscious diners while the dessert tray satisfies anyone with a passionate sweet tooth. Highlights are chocolate desserts, cheesecake, cappuccino mousse pie and cake and an almond cookie shell filled with vanilla bean creme brulee.

Specialties include Snapper La Griglia; Lacquer Chicken, which is marinated in herbs, glazed with honey and served with morel mushrooms and Parmesan mashed potatoes; Katsy Burger, a grilled portobello mushroom burger; Shrimp and Crab Cheesecake with seafood sauce; Margherita Pizza and Peking Pizza topped with duck, shiitake mushrooms and oriental plum sauce.

Anthony's
4007 Westheimer
Houston, Tx 77027
961-0552

─── LITE FARE ───

Both these superb restaurants reflect Tony Vallone's philosophy that delicious dining can be healthy as well. Dishes use special low-fat cooking preparation that concentrates flavor. Special Spa Selections at La Griglia feature low-sodium, fat and calorie entrees. At Anthony's look for daily Spa specials. Special requests are welcomed and honored.

La Griglia
2002 W. Gray
Houston, Tx 77019
526-4700

ANTHONY'S SEARED SHRIMP *with Spicy Mango Salsa*

1/4	cup oil
16	large shrimp (16/20 count), peeled and deveined, tails on
1/4	cup each, diced: yellow onion and red and green bell peppers
1/2	cup diced Bosc or Anjou pears
3	ounces pineapple juice
1/4	cup each, diced: red onion and firm red tomato
2	large ripe mangos, peeled, seeded and diced
1 1/2	teaspoons seeded, finely diced serrano peppers
1/4	cup finely chopped fresh mint Salt and freshly ground black pepper to taste
2	lemons Fresh mint for garnish

Heat oil in a large skillet until very hot. Add shrimp; cook 2 minutes. Add yellow onion; cook until shrimp are done.

Add bell peppers, pear and pineapple juice; cook 1 minute. Remove from heat. Add red onion, tomato, mangos, serranos, mint, salt and pepper to taste. Squeeze lemon over top; garnish with mint.

Serves 4.

Serving Suggestion: Serve with spinach sauteed with garlic and a little olive oil. Garnish with bouquet of red tip lettuce, curly endive, radicchio and fennel tied with chives (dip chives in hot water to soften).

Cut oil to 1 tablespoon for sauteing.

Kendall-Jackson Chardonnay Vintner's Reserve; Schloss Johannisberg Riesling Spatlese (Germany); Preston Viognier.

BLACKBERRY CRUSTADE

2	cups plus 2 tablespoons all-purpose flour, divided
1 1/4	cups sugar, divided
1	cup (2 sticks) very cold butter, cut into 1/4-inch squares Pinch of salt
1/4	cup ice water
2	cups fresh blackberries
1	teaspoon ground cinnamon Topping (recipe follows)

TOPPING

1/2	cup (1 stick) butter
1/4	cup each: sugar and all-purpose flour

Preheat oven to 350 degrees. Mix 2 cups flour, 1/4 cup sugar, butter and salt in medium bowl until butter is incorporated. Add water and knead until dough cleans the sides of the bowl. Dust hands and board lightly with flour. Roll dough out to 1/8-inch thick, cut into four (6 1/2-inch) circles. Arrange in four (4-inch) fluted tart pans.

Mix berries with remaining 1 cup sugar, 2 tablespoons flour and cinnamon; divide among tart pans and pull corners up to partially cover berries. Add topping. Bake 45 minutes, or until golden brown.

Topping: Combine butter, sugar and flour in food processor bowl. Pulse 5 seconds; repeat; mixture will be crumbly. Sprinkle over top of berry tarts.

Serves 4.

Serving Suggestion: Serve with mango and blackberry sauces and vanilla ice cream. Garnish with berries.

Share this dessert with a friend.

Chateau St. Jean Late Harvest Riesling; Schloss Vollrads Beerenauslese or Eiswein (Germany); Chateau Rieussec (France).

SNAPPER LA GRIGLIA

Champagne Sauce (recipe
follows)
4 (8-ounce) red snapper fillets
1/4 cup extra-virgin olive oil
3 cups cooked risotto, formed
into 4 cakes

GARNISH:
1/2 bunch fresh spinach, cleaned
and cooked;
4 small bunches champagne
grapes;
4 crab claws boiled in seasoned
water; cut chives for garnish

CHAMPAGNE SAUCE
1 finely diced shallot
1/2 cup champagne
Juice of 2 lemons
1/4 cup whipping cream
1/2 cup (1 stick) butter
Salt and freshly ground black
pepper to taste
1 cup jumbo lump crabmeat,
picked over

Make Champagne Sauce; set aside. Sear snapper fillets in hot oil in a skillet 3 minutes per side.

To serve, place a snapper fillet and 1 risotto cake on each plate. Pour Champagne Sauce over snapper. Garnish each plate with spinach, grapes, crab claw and chives.

Champagne Sauce
Place shallot and champagne in a 1-quart saucepan. Cook over medium heat until reduced by two-thirds. Add lemon juice; simmer a few minutes. Whisk in cream and butter. Adjust seasoning with salt and pepper. Add crabmeat; set aside.

Serves 4.

🍎 Use just 1 tablespoon oil for sauteing. In the Champagne Sauce, cut butter to 1/4 cup and substitute half-and-half for cream. Use salt-free, defatted chicken stock to prepare risotto.

🍇 Domaine de Chardonnay Clos Barry (France); Belvedere Chardonnay; M. Colin-Deleger, Bernard Morey or Michel Niellon Chassagne-Montrachet (France).

JOEY'S NUTTY SALAD

1/4 cup each, chopped: pine nuts (pignolia), pecans, walnuts and hazelnuts
1 tablespoon sugar
1 tablespoon extra-virgin olive oil
2 tablespoons honey
1/4 teaspoon salt
Pinch of ground white pepper
Honey Balsamic Dressing (recipe follows)
Caramelized Onions (recipe follows)
2 cups each: fresh spinach leaves, red oak leaf lettuce and arugula
1/2 cup each: radicchio and watercress
1/4 cup goat cheese, crumbled

HONEY BALSAMIC DRESSING
1 egg (optional)
1 cup extra-virgin olive oil
2 tablespoons honey
1 garlic clove, minced
3 tablespoons balsamic vinegar (dark, aged Italian vinegar)

CARAMELIZED ONIONS
2 tablespoons extra-virgin olive oil
1 cup thinly sliced yellow onion
2 tablespoons honey
1 tablespoon balsamic vinegar

Preheat oven to 250 degrees. In mixing bowl, toss pine nuts, pecans, walnuts and hazelnuts with sugar, oil and honey. Season with salt and pepper. Place seasoned nuts on a baking pan in a single layer and roast until golden brown, 8 to 10 minutes. Remove from oven and let cool.

Prepare Honey Balsamic Dressing and Caramelized Onions.

For greens, remove discolored leaves and stems; wash twice thoroughly in ice-cold water. Drain dry; chill. Tear into large, bite-size pieces. Place chilled mixed greens in a salad bowl.

To assemble: Toss greens and roasted nuts with 1 cup Honey Balsamic Dressing. Divide greens among salad plates and sprinkle with cheese and Caramelized Onions.

Honey Balsamic Dressing
Lightly whisk egg (if used), then gradually whisk in oil, honey, garlic and vinegar.

Note: If concerned about using a raw egg, use an equivalent amount of egg substitute.

Caramelized Onions
Heat oil in skillet over medium heat; sauté onion until golden brown, 7 to 8 minutes. Stirring constantly, whisk in honey and vinegar. Sauté until onions are caramelized; set aside.

Serves 4.

Cut nuts to 1/4 cup and eliminate oil in preparing nuts. Make Honey Balsamic Dressing with 1/2 cup oil, using 1 tablespoon per serving. Reduce oil in Caramelized Onions to 1 tablespoon.

Buehler White Zinfandel; Navarro Gewurztraminer; Trefethen White Riesling.

TEXAS CREOLE BARBECUE SHRIMP
with Jicama Salad and Texas Cornbread Pudding
CHOCOLATE PEANUT BUTTER FUDGE PIE
MAMA'S CARROT CAKE
THIRD COAST CRABCAKES
with Lemon Butter Sauce & Pico de Gallo

Brennan's will celebrate 30 years of standard-setting hospitality and fine dining in 1997 by expanding its kitchen and its culinary horizons. Weekend jazz brunches, New Orleans ambiance and special features such as dining at the Kitchen Table in the bustling kitchen place Brennan's high on the list of Houston favorites. For many customers it is "the" place to celebrate life's champagne occasions, entertain clients at lunch and dinner, have a drink at the bar (one of the best in the city), meet for a romantic rendezvous or after-theater dining.

Its forward-looking Texas-Creole Cuisine continues to evolve under the direction of Alex Brennan-Martin and executive chef Carl Walker. The food overlays New Orleans tradition with the taste of fresh Texas and regional ingredients — jambalaya teams up with risotto; crawfish becomes a filling for enchiladas; amberjack, cobia (ling) fish, yellow-edge grouper, tombo (Hawaiian albacore) and other exotic and farmed fish go swimmingly with Creole sauces and salsas. For today's diners who just want "a bite of dessert" for special occasions, the chef might arrange five spoons with a bite each of five desserts on a plate with a demitasse of souffle as lagniappe. Wines from Brennan's extensive wine collection provide the finishing touch.

Third Coast (referring to the Gulf Coast), a more casual restaurant owned by Brennan-Martin and acclaimed Houston restaurateurs Bruce and Susan Molzan of Ruggles, also specializes in fish and seafood along with rotisserie and grilled entrees and homestyle dishes such as meat loaf and carrot cake. Lunch specials include inventive grilled tuna and crab cake sandwiches.

As interpreted by chef Russell Knott, Third Coast provides "exciting food you can eat every day." Three heart-healthy spa specials are featured nightly. Use of butter and cream is minimal, especially in popular vegetable dishes such as the best-selling Outrageous Vegetable Plate. Flavor comes from sun-dried tomatoes, chilies, goat cheese, and fresh herbs and greens from a local herb farm.

The restaurant is a popular neighborhood gathering place, especially the glass-enclosed patio. A wine room and "library" are available for small private parties.

─────────── LITE FARE ───────────

Healthy dining is a dedication of both these superior restaurants. Brennan's Lite-Hearted Selections offer deliciously healthy appetizers, entrees and desserts, while Third Coast marks items for health conscious diners with a "thumbs-up" symbol. These items are prepared with no cream or butter and very little oil, but an abundance of fresh flavors.

Brennan's
3300 Smith St.
Houston, Tx 77006
522-9711

Third Coast
6540 San Felipe
Houston, Tx 77057
783-6540

TEXAS CREOLE BARBECUE SHRIMP

1/2 tablespoon vegetable oil
1/2 each, julienned: red bell and poblano peppers, yellow onion
3/4 teaspoon chopped garlic
1 pound large shrimp (16/20 count), peeled and deveined
3/4 cup Barbecue Sauce Base (recipe follows)
1/4 cup whipping cream
Jicama Salad
Texas Cornbread Pudding

BARBECUE SAUCE BASE

2 1/2 medium lemons, peeled and quartered
3 tablespoons freshly ground black pepper
2 tablespoons seafood seasoning
1 cup each: Worcestershire sauce and water
6 garlic cloves

JICAMA SALAD

1 1/2 cups peeled, julienned jicama
Juice of 1 lime
Salt and freshly ground black pepper to taste

TEXAS CORNBREAD PUDDING

1 tablespoon vegetable oil
1/2 cup diced yellow onion
1 1/2 cups fresh cut corn
4 eggs
2 cups whipping cream
1 recipe (1 quart) cornbread, diced
1 cup shredded jalapeno jack cheese, divided
Salt and freshly ground black pepper to taste
1 fresh jalapeno, thinly sliced

Heat oil in a large skillet; sauté bell pepper, poblano, onion and garlic about 30 to 40 seconds. Add shrimp and sauté 30 seconds. Stir in Barbecue Sauce Base and bring to a simmer. Blend in cream and simmer until shrimp are cooked, about 5 minutes. Do not overcook.

Spoon shrimp and sauce onto plate and serve with Texas Cornbread Pudding and Jicama Salad.

Barbecue Sauce Base

Combine lemons, pepper, seafood seasoning, Worcestershire, water and garlic in a saucepan; cook until reduced by half. Strain and use for barbecue shrimp. Adjust spiciness of sauce by increasing or decreasing to your taste.

Jicama Salad

Season jicama with lime juice, salt and pepper. The jicama gives a refreshing taste to the spicy shrimp.

Texas Cornbread Pudding

Preheat oven to 300 degrees. Heat oil in a medium skillet; sauté onion and corn until translucent. Combine eggs and cream in a large bowl; blend in cornbread, corn mixture and 1/2 cup cheese. Season with salt and pepper.

Butter an 8x8x2-inch pan or spray with nonstick spray. Pour in custard mixture. Sprinkle top with remaining 1/2 cup cheese and jalapeno slices. Set pan in water bath (a larger pan of hot water that comes to within 1/2-inch of top of baking pan). Bake 1 hour, or until firm.

Serves 4 to 6.

Skip the Texas Cornbread Pudding and enjoy the barbecue shrimp.

Canyon Road Sauvignon-Blanc; Sancerre Clos de la Crele (France); Caymus Conundrum.

CHOCOLATE PEANUT BUTTER FUDGE PIE

Created for the Republican Convention held in Houston in 1992.

1   cup chunky peanut butter
1   (9-inch) chocolate cookie crust
5   tablespoons unsalted butter, melted
8   ounces semi-sweet chocolate, melted
3   eggs, separated
4   tablespoons sugar, divided
6 1/2   tablespoons each: unsalted dry-roasted peanuts, semisweet and white chocolate chunks
1   cup whipping cream (chill cream, bowl and beaters thoroughly) Chocolate sauce, caramel sauce and chopped unsalted peanuts for garnish

Spread peanut butter over bottom of pie crust; set aside. Fold butter into melted chocolate; set aside. Beat egg yolks and 2 tablespoons sugar until thick and pale yellow. Fold into chocolate mixture. In clean dry bowl and clean beaters, whip egg whites to soft peaks and add remaining 2 tablespoons sugar; whip to stiff peaks. Fold into chocolate mixture.

Fold peanuts, dark and white chocolate chunks into chocolate mixture. Spread over peanut butter in pie shell; level. Refrigerate pie until set, about 2 hours. Five minutes before serving, whip cream. Top pie with whipped cream. Drizzle with chocolate and caramel sauces; sprinkle with peanuts.

Serves 6 to 8.

MAMA'S CARROT CAKE

Florence C. Gibson has been making this spectacular four-layer cake at Brennan's for 22 years. It's also one of the most popular desserts at Third Coast.

8   eggs
3   cups corn oil
1   tablespoon vanilla
4   cups leveled brown sugar, not packed
4   cups all-purpose flour
2   teaspoons each: ground cinnamon and baking soda
1   teaspoon salt
3   cups finely grated carrots
     Mama's Carrot Cake Icing

MAMA'S CARROT CAKE ICING

3   (3-ounce) packages chilled cream cheese, not straight from refrigerator
1/2   cup (1 stick) unsalted butter
1   tablespoon vanilla
4   cups powdered sugar (1 pound)
1/4   cup chopped pecans
1/4   cup grated carrots (optional)

Preheat oven to 325 degrees. Beat eggs, oil and vanilla together in large electric mixer bowl. Blend in sugar. Combine flour, cinnamon, soda and salt; add to mixture. Stir in carrots. Pour into four greased, floured (9-inch) layer cake pans and fill three-fourths full. Bake about 40 to 45 minutes. Remove from pan; cool completely. Ice with Mama's Carrot Cake Icing.

Note: At the restaurant, any cake that rises above the rim of the pan is cut off level with a serrated knife. It is considered a delicacy by the staff and is sometimes used in bread pudding.

Mama's Carrot Cake Icing

Beat cream cheese and butter together in electric mixer. Blend in vanilla. Add sugar gradually, beating until smooth. Stir in pecans and carrots. Frost cake between layers, frost sides and top of cake. Store covered in refrigerator.

Serves 12 to 16.

THIRD COAST CRABCAKES
with Lemon Butter Sauce & Pico de Gallo

2	tablespoons extra-virgin olive oil
1/2	cup each, diced: yellow onion and green and red bell peppers
2	tablespoons minced garlic
2	tablespoons each: Creole mustard and Worcestershire sauce
	Salt to taste
1/2	tablespoon (1 1/2 teaspoons) freshly ground black pepper
1/2	teaspoon cayenne pepper
1/2	cup dry plain bread crumbs
2	eggs, lightly beaten
1 1/2	pounds jumbo lump crabmeat
1/2	cup thinly sliced green onions
	Lemon Butter Sauce (recipe follows)
	Pico de Gallo (recipe follows)

LEMON BUTTER SAUCE

1	lemon, peeled and quartered
1	shallot, minced
1/4	cup dry white wine
1	bay leaf
1 1/2	teaspoons whole black peppercorns
1	pound (4 sticks) unsalted butter, cut into pieces
1	teaspoon salt
1/4	teaspoon white pepper

PICO DE GALLO

1	cup diced Roma tomatoes
1/4	cup diced yellow onion
1/4	cup fresh cilantro leaves
1	tablespoon minced garlic
2	tablespoons fresh lemon juice
1	tablespoon fresh lime juice
1	teaspoon salt
1/4	teaspoon freshly ground black pepper

Heat oil in a 10-inch skillet; sauté onion, bell peppers and garlic until tender. Combine vegetables with mustard, Worcestershire, salt, pepper and cayenne in a medium bowl. Blend in bread crumbs and eggs. Stir in crabmeat and green onion. Form into 12 patties (about 2 inches in diameter and 1-inch thick).

Sauté patties in same skillet over medium heat until golden brown, about 30 seconds (additional oil may be needed). Keep warm in 200-degree oven.

Presentation: Place Lemon Butter Sauce on plate; add 3 crabcakes per serving and top with Pico de Gallo.

Lemon Butter Sauce

Combine lemon, shallot, wine, bay leaf and peppercorns in a heavy bottom saucepan; cook over medium heat until reduced to almost dry. Whisk in several pieces butter at a time; season with salt and white pepper. Remove bay leaf; set aside.

Pico de Gallo

Combine tomatoes, onion, cilantro, garlic, juices, salt and pepper. Set aside.

Serves 4.

Skip the Lemon Butter Sauce and enjoy the crabcakes with Pico de Gallo.

Chateau St. Jean Fume-Blanc La Petite Etoile; Lacour Pavillon Blanc (France); Pouilly-Fuisse Verget (France); Puligny-Montrachet Domaine Leflaive Les Combettes, Les Folatieres or Les Pucelles (France).

SWEET POTATO CHIPOTLE BISQUE
GRILLED CARIBBEAN SHRIMP
with Cuban Barbecue Sauce and Orange-Jalapeno Risotto
GRILLED QUAIL AND PORTOBELLO MUSHROOM SALAD

The Brownstone, a one-of-a-kind restaurant that opened in 1973, blends southern and continental charm with New World Cuisine. A shaded courtyard with graceful statues and fountains welcomes you to a lushly decorated home-like setting filled with intimate dining areas. It is a tour de force for owner Beau Theriot, an interior designer, who filled the restaurant with antiques, original paintings, Baccarat crystal chandeliers and fine tableware.

You can choose a venue to suit your mood — the wine room is perfect for small dinner parties; several private rooms can accommodate everything from an intimate dinner for two or a birthday gathering to a large corporate party or wedding rehearsal dinner. A richly appointed dining area with a paisley-tented ceiling can be the setting for a light-hearted luncheon or dinner party. The outdoor patio, with its swimming pool and cabana, accommodates 100 for a cocktail party. To add to the atmosphere, a pianist plays at lunch Monday through Saturday and at dinner on Wednesdays, and a harpist provides background music Thursday through Saturday nights.

If your taste leans to elegant, traditional dishes such as Beef Wellington and Chateaubriand, you'll find them here along with The Brownstone's timeless Avocado Velvet Soup. But the talented young chef, Douglas Bass, is introducing diners to exciting new culinary adventures.

Bass, who holds a degree in physics from Texas A&M University, says he sees a strong connection between the precision and complexity of science and fine cooking. A life-long interest in food caused him to make a career change after graduation. He decided to become a chef and enrolled in the Pennsylvania Institute of Culinary Arts.

Since moving here in 1995, Bass says Houston's different ethnic influences have challenged him to compose multi-faceted dishes. His New World Cuisine combines elements of Caribbean, Asian, Italian, Mexican, Southern and Southwestern cooking in such dishes as Serrano Chile Seared Sea Scallops with Saffron Risotto and Lemon-Thyme Essence; and Ginger Spiced Peking Duck, Hibachi Rice and Stir-Fried Vegetables with Sake-Plum Sauce. Bass also pays homage to the Brownstone's Creole roots with Blackened Chicken Breast with fettuccine, peppers, tomatoes and a Creole Alfredo Sauce.

LITE FARE

The Brownstone has moved to light, healthy food preparation and sauces with Healthy Alternative menu items. Enjoy the Apple Braised Salmon, Charred Tuna Pasta with a Plum Tomato Sauce or Wasabi Seared Ahi Tuna with Basmati Rice. All herbs and vegetables are fresh. Fruit sorbets and berries make a sweet ending to a delicious meal.

The Brownstone
2736 Virginia
Houston, Tx 77098
520-5666

SWEET POTATO-CHIPOTLE BISQUE

1	tablespoon clarified butter
1/2	cup finely diced yellow onion
1/4	cup each, finely diced: celery and carrots
1/4	cup minced garlic
3	large sweet potatoes, peeled and cut into large chunks
1	chipotle chile, seeded
2	quarts chicken stock
1	cup white wine
1/2	tablespoon (1 1/2 teaspoons) each: ground cumin and coriander
1/2	teaspoon each: ground nutmeg and allspice
2	cups whipping cream Salt and freshly ground black pepper to taste

Heat butter in a large saucepan. Sauté onion, celery, carrots, garlic, potatoes and chipotle until partially cooked. Add stock, wine, cumin, coriander, nutmeg and allspice. Simmer until potatoes are done, about 30 to 45 minutes.

In batches, puree soup in blender until smooth. Return to stock pot; stir in cream, salt and pepper. Heat to serving temperature.

Serves 8.

 Use salt-free, defatted chicken stock. Substitute evaporated skim milk for cream.

Fall Creek Emerald Riesling (Texas); Trefethen White Riesling; Caymus Conundrum.

GRILLED CARIBBEAN SHRIMP
with Cuban Barbecue Sauce and Orange-Jalapeno Risotto

2	cups olive oil
1	yellow onion, chopped
3	Scotch Bonnet chilies, seeded and chopped
1	tablespoon minced garlic
1	tablespoon each: allspice, cardamom, coriander, ginger, nutmeg, basil leaves, fresh chives and thyme
1	teaspoon each: ground cinnamon, salt and freshly ground black pepper
1/4	cup dark soy sauce
24	large shrimp (16/20 count), peeled and deveined Cuban Barbecue Sauce (recipe follows) Orange-Jalapeno Risotto (recipe follows) Chopped fresh parsley for garnish

Combine oil, onion, chilies, garlic, allspice, cardamom, coriander, ginger, nutmeg, basil, chives, thyme, cinnamon, salt, pepper and soy sauce in food processor or blender; puree. Pour over shrimp in medium bowl; cover and refrigerate 24 hours. Remove shrimp from marinade, and grill as desired.

To serve, place a mound of risotto in center of each plate. Surround risotto with sauce and place 2 shrimp on each side. Garnish with parsley.

CUBAN BARBECUE SAUCE

1	cup cooked black beans, drained
1	cup chopped onion
1/2	cup chopped red bell pepper
1/4	cup chopped cilantro leaves
1	tablespoon chopped garlic
1	tablespoon minced fresh ginger
3	each, chopped: mangos and large Roma tomatoes
2	jalapenos, seeded, deveined and chopped
1	chipotle chile, seeded and chopped
1	cup chicken stock
1/2	cup honey
1/4	cup rice wine vinegar
1	teaspoon each, ground: allspice, cardamom, coriander, cumin, curry powder, nutmeg and thyme Salt and freshly ground black pepper to taste

Cuban Barbecue Sauce

Place beans, onion, bell pepper, cilantro, garlic, ginger, mangos, tomatoes, jalapenos, chipotle, stock, honey, vinegar, allspice, cardamom, coriander, cumin, curry powder, nutmeg, thyme, salt and pepper in a 2 1/2-quart saucepan over medium heat. Cook until vegetables are soft, about 10 minutes, over medium-low heat. Puree in batches in blender until smooth.

ORANGE-JALAPENO RISOTTO

3	tablespoons butter, divided
1	cup finely chopped yellow onion
1	tablespoon chopped garlic
1	cup Arborio rice
1	cup dry white wine
2	cups chicken stock
1	cup fresh orange juice
5	jalapenos, seeded, deveined and chopped Salt and freshly ground black pepper to taste
1/4	cup freshly grated Parmesan cheese

Orange-Jalapeno Risotto

Heat 1 tablespoon butter in a saucepan over medium heat. Sauté onion and garlic until softened. Stir in rice; cook until toasted aroma develops, about 3 to 4 minutes. Add wine; stir.

Add stock and orange juice, 1/2 cup at a time, and cook over low heat until all liquid is absorbed, stirring constantly. Stir in jalapenos, salt and pepper. Set aside. Just before serving, stir in remaining 2 tablespoons butter and Parmesan.

Serves 6.

 Delicious and healthy recipe. Enjoy!

Santa Alicia Chardonnay Reserve (Chile); Wynne's Coonawarra Chardonnay (Australia); Byron or Au Bon Climat Chardonnay.

GRILLED QUAIL AND PORTOBELLO MUSHROOM SALAD

2 boneless quail
1 portobello mushroom cap, sliced
1 cup olive oil
1 tablespoon each, chopped: garlic and mixed fresh herbs (thyme, basil, chives, oregano and a touch of dill)
  Dressing (recipe follows)
1 red onion, thinly sliced
  Burgundy wine
  Mesclun greens or field salad to serve 2
2 each: red and yellow teardrop tomatoes
1/2 cup crumbled Gorgonzola cheese
2 tablespoons toasted pumpkin seeds

DRESSING

1/2 cup balsamic vinegar
2 tablespoons chopped fresh mixed herbs
1 tablespoon each, chopped: garlic and shallots
1 cup olive oil
  Salt and freshly ground black pepper to taste

Marinate quail and mushroom in oil, garlic and herbs covered in refrigerator 8 hours. Remove from marinade; grill quail and mushroom over charcoal with a few mesquite chips 5 minutes per side.

Prepare dressing. Simmer onion in Burgundy wine to cover until softened, about 10 minutes. Toss greens with dressing; arrange on plate. Add onion, tomatoes and cheese. Slice quail; arrange around salad with mushroom slices. Garnish with pumpkin seeds.

Dressing

Combine vinegar, herbs, garlic and shallots in small bowl. Slowly whisk in oil to create an emulsion; add salt and pepper. Makes enough dressing for 6.

Serves 2.

Eliminate pumpkin seeds. Cut cheese and dressing to 2 tablespoons each per serving. Remove skin from quail before eating.

Villa Montes or Montes Merlot (Chile); Duboeuf Julienas, Morgon, Fleurie or Moulin-a-Vent (France); Beaune Jadot (France); Corton Meo-Camuzet or Jadot (France).

FACING PAGE, FROM LEFT: *Carlos O. Castellanos, Churrascos; J. M. Matos, Deco at the Adams Mark; Humberto Molina-Segura, Americas.*
FOLLOWING PAGE, FROM LEFT: *Massoud Bastankhah, Cafe Caspian; Denman Moody, Wine Connoisseur; Russell Knott, Third Coast; Carl Walker, Brennan's.*

YOGURT AND SPINACH DIP
CHICKEN KABAB
RICE WITH LIMA BEANS

Although Persian restaurants have only recently arrived on the Houston dining scene, the cuisine dates back 3,000 years, to a time when recipes for traditional dishes were inscribed on clay tablets. The food charmed even the Persian Empire's conquerers such as Alexander the Great. His soldiers carried home exotic foods that later worked their way into Greek and Roman cooking and throughout the Mediterranean.

Cafe Caspian is foremost among the restaurants introducing Houston to the pleasures of the Persian table. There are many, especially for those who enjoy flavors and textures without the intense heat of chilies and seasonings found in many other favored ethnic cuisines.

Cafe Caspian

Popular dishes include a variety of basmati rice preparations, beef and vegetable stews, chicken, fish, lamb, lentils, eggplant, spinach and yogurt-cooled relishes. Seasonings — sumac, saffron, cardamom, turmeric, cinnamon, parsley, mint, barberries and rose water — may seem curious at first, but are a quick guide to the distinctive tastes of Persian cuisine just as cilantro and chilies are to Latin cooking. Barberries — zereshk — are small red dried sour fruits that somewhat resemble raisins or currants. Cranberries are another possible substitute.

There could be no better introduction to Persian food than Cafe Caspian's complimentary platter of sabzi khordan — fresh herbs, greens, radishes, onion and feta cheese to assemble as you like and wrap in warm taftoon bread. The flat rounds of bread are slapped against the sides of the tandoori oven to bake and are timed so the bread is always warm when it arrives at your table.

Cafe Caspian's best-of-the-best combination dinners also educate your palate. Almost all are served with basmati rice, which is steamed in a unique way so that it forms a golden crust at the bottom of the pot. The crust is a highly prized delicacy; it is often heated and eaten for breakfast with milk and jam or served cold with cheese and garlic. Traditionally Persian rice is soaked and washed five times, but this is not necessary when using American long-grain or Texmati rice.

Cafe Caspian serves Houston's large Iranian population of about 54,000 and frequently caters ceremonial occasions such as weddings and funerals, said owner Massoud "Max" Bastankhah.

LITE FARE

Cafe Caspian combines the healthful cuisines of the Mediterranean and the Middle East. Fresh herbs, vegetables, rice, lean meats and seafood are combined with low-fat cooking methods of grilling and steaming. Yogurt is used to bind sauces and dips. All dishes are served with basmati rice, a complex carbohydrate with a nut-like flavor.

Cafe Caspian
2730 Hillcroft
Houston, Tx 77057
266-4900

YOGURT AND SPINACH DIP – BORANI ESFENAJ

8	cups fresh leaf spinach, washed and chopped, or 2 cups frozen, thawed
4	tablespoons olive oil
2	medium-size white onions, thinly sliced
5	garlic cloves, crushed
3	cups plain yogurt (can use nonfat)
1	teaspoon salt
1/2	teaspoon freshly ground black pepper
	Fresh mint for garnish

Steam spinach in a saucepan over medium heat 10 to 12 minutes, or until wilted; drain. Heat oil in skillet; sauté onion and garlic until lightly browned; stir in spinach and sauté 2 more minutes. Remove from heat and cool.

In serving bowl, mix yogurt with spinach; season with salt and pepper. Refrigerate several hours before serving. Garnish with mint.

Serves 8.

Use nonfat yogurt and decrease oil to 2 tablespoons. Great as a dip for raw vegetables.

Beringer White Zinfandel; Fall Creek Chenin Blanc (Texas); Duboeuf Viognier (France).

CHICKEN KABAB – JOO-JEH KABAB

1 teaspoon ground saffron
2 tablespoons hot water
1 cup fresh lime juice
   Juice of 2 onions (see note)
2 tablespoons olive oil
1 teaspoon salt
2 (24-ounce) Cornish hens, cut
   into pieces
4 large tomatoes, cut into
   quarters
   Basting Sauce (recipe follows)

BASTING SAUCE

   Juice of 1 lime
2 tablespoons butter
1 teaspoon each: salt and freshly
   ground black pepper

Dissolve saffron in hot water in small custard cup. In large bowl, combine 1 teaspoon saffron water with lime and onion juices, oil and salt. Beat well with fork. Add Cornish hen pieces, cover and marinate in refrigerator 4 to 6 hours or overnight.

Start charcoal at least 30 minutes before you plan to cook; let burn until coals glow evenly to a gray ash. Or, preheat oven broiler.

Place tomatoes on skewers; set aside. Place Cornish hen legs on rack over charcoal first, then breasts, thighs and wings. Turn occasionally and baste 3 to 4 times during cooking with Basting Sauce. Grill 10 to 15 minutes. Add skewers of tomatoes during last 4 to 5 minutes of grilling. When hens are done (juices should be clear), serve immediately with basmati rice and garnish with fresh herbs.

Note: Grind and strain onions to yield 1/2 cup juice.

Basting Sauce

Combine remaining saffron water, lime juice, butter, salt and pepper; mix well.

Serves 2.

Remove skin from Cornish hens before eating. Decrease butter and oil to 1 tablespoon each. Eliminate added salt.

White: SIMI or Robert Mondavi Fume-Blanc; Kendall-Jackson Chardonnay Grand Reserve; Maculan Chardonnay (Italy).

Red: Chianti Classico Brolio (Italy); Chanti Classico Riserva San Felice (Italy); Brunello di Montalcino Banfi or Argiano (Italy).

RICE WITH LIMA BEANS

3 cups basmati rice
8 cups water
2 tablespoons salt
1 1/2 teaspoons ground saffron
2 tablespoons hot water
3/4 cup (1 1/2 sticks) butter, divided
1/2 cup hot water
1 (16-ounce) package frozen lima beans, thawed
6 cups fresh finely chopped dill weed (see note)
4 garlic cloves, chopped

Bring water and salt to boil in 3-quart Teflon-coated saucepan. Add rice; boil 10 minutes, gently stirring with wooden spoon to loosen any grains that may stick to bottom. When rice feels soft and tender inside, drain and rinse in lukewarm water.

Combine saffron and hot water in small custard cup. In same saucepan, heat 1/2 cup butter with a few drops of saffron water, which will create a golden crust (tah dig) when rice is cooked. Mix rice, lima beans, dill weed and garlic together; place over butter mixture and shape into a pyramid, leaving room for rice to expand and enlarge. Cover and cook over medium heat 10 minutes to form golden crust.

Dissolve remaining 1/4 cup butter in hot water; pour over rice. Place a linen kitchen towel over rice and cover tightly with lid. Cook 40 to 50 minutes. Remove from heat; allow to cool 5 minutes.

Put 2 tablespoons of cooked rice in a small dish; mix with remaining saffron water and set aside for garnish.

Gently remove rice and arrange mounds onto individual plates. Sprinkle saffron rice garnish over top of each. Detach layer of crust from bottom of pan using a wooden spatula. Place on a platter and serve on the side.

Note: In her book, "New Food of Life," Najmieh Batmanglij says if you must use dried herbs, reduce amount to one-fourth of the fresh herbs. Place dried dill in a sieve in a bowl of lukewarm water and soak 15 minutes. Remove from sieve and use as directed.

Serves 6 to 8.

Reduce salt to 2 teaspoons and butter to 1/2 cup. Makes 9 (1-cup) servings.

Commanderie de la Bargemone (France); Trimbach Pinot Blanc (France); Chalone Pinot Blanc.

INSALATA DEL CUOCO
MARINARA SAUCE
RIGATONI ALLA VERDURE
SCALLOPINI DI POLLO

Birthdays, anniversaries, business luncheons, romantic dinners for two, lunch for friends or out-of-town company — those are only a few of the 'remember when' occasions that make Cavatore memorable.

Loyal fans also have their perennial menu favorites — Fettuccine Carbonara and Alfredo; fried calamari; seafood lasagna; Penne alla Mafia made with fresh sausage; Veal Francese, Veal Milanese, Chicken Scallopini and Chicken With Rosemary; and Eggplant Parmigiana. Desserts include cannoli and Tiramisu Genovese, a classic tiramisu preparation of Italian ladyfingers soaked in espresso and brandy layered with mascarpone cheese and custard. A newly popular dessert is chocolate mousse presented in a tulip-shaped cup of dark chocolate or white chocolate mousse in a white chocolate tulip cup.

Chef Greg Torres also offers several low-calorie and grilled specials. The ample wine list includes a large selection of Italian wines including Barolos and nine Chianti Riservas.

The building itself — a 100-year-old barn that the owners found in Bastrop, Texas — is an "only in Houston" conversation piece. It was transported here to a location across the street from La Tour d'Argent, also owned by the same partners, Giancarlo Cavatore and Sonny Lahham. They repaired the barn and painstakingly reconstructed it as close to the original as possible, adding a covered deck overlooking a waterfall pond stocked with goldfish. Inside there is a virtual museum of antique Italian movie posters, vintage newspapers and photographs, flags and Italian memorabilia.

The colorful menu cover with its cartoon map of Columbus sailing toward America in a boat heaped with foodstuffs also is a conversation piece. Photos of historic figures, friends, family and even family pets are worked into the collage. The restaurant logo, a composite of Italian, American and Texas flags punctuated with a stylized Lone Star, is another design theme. It appears in stained glass windows and adorns waiters' aprons and matchbook covers.

ITALIAN CAVATORE RESTAURANT

Music adds to the festive atmosphere and says the party is just waiting on you to begin. A pianist plays nightly except Sunday. Several private rooms can accommodate parties of from 10 to 180.

LITE FARE

Enjoy the Chef's Special Low Calorie section for dishes prepared with a minimum of oil and loads of taste. Pastas come in appetizer and regular sizes; great for portion control. Accompany with minestrone soup or salad. Pastas are also divided into "fresh" which usually contain eggs that add fat and cholesterol and "dry", which are relatively fat-free.

Cavatore
2120 Ella Blvd.
Houston, Tx 77008
869-6622

INSALATA DEL CUOCO

16   large shrimp (16/20 count)
4   garlic cloves, finely minced
3   teaspoons chopped fresh basil
1   teaspoon finely chopped fresh parsley
4   tablespoons extra-virgin olive oil
     Salt and freshly ground black pepper to taste
2   hearts of Romaine lettuce, cut in half lengthwise
6   ounces white mushrooms, stemmed and sliced
2   teaspoons balsamic vinegar
8   artichoke hearts (if using canned, drain)
8   Kalamata olives
2   tomatoes, cut in wedges

Peel and boil shrimp just until it turns pink. Drain and marinate covered overnight in the refrigerator in a mixture of garlic, basil, parsley, oil, salt and pepper.

To serve, place a Romaine half on each of 4 plates. Remove shrimp from marinade; reserve marinade. Arrange shrimp and mushrooms on top.

Whisk 2 teaspoons balsamic vinaigrette (see note) into reserved marinade. Spoon over shrimp and mushrooms. Garnish with artichoke hearts, olives and tomato wedges.

Note: Use your favorite vinaigrette recipe made with balsamic vinegar.

Serves 4.

 Reduce oil to just 1 tablespoon.

Verdicchio Fazi-Battaglia (Italy); Hess Select Chardonnay; Peter Michael or St. Francis Chardonnay.

MARINARA SAUCE

1/2 cup extra-virgin olive oil
8   large garlic cloves, chopped
16   large ripe Roma tomatoes, peeled, chopped and drained
1   teaspoon crushed red pepper flakes
     Pinch of sugar
     Salt to taste
4   tablespoons chopped fresh basil
2   tablespoons sliced green onion

Heat oil in large skillet. Sauté garlic until it begins to color. Add tomatoes; cook until all excess liquid evaporates. Add pepper flakes, sugar and salt. Cook 7 minutes. Add basil and onion. Serve over pasta of choice.

Serves 4.

Reduce oil to 2 tablespoons and serve with 1 cup of pasta. Great source of vitamins A and C.

Ceretto Dolcetto d'Alba (Italy); Tenute Chianti Classico Riserva Antinori (Italy); Ornellaia (Italy).

RIGATONI ALLA VERDURE

1   pound dry rigatoni pasta
12   ounces sliced boneless veal
12   large shrimp (16/20 count)
      All-purpose flour
5   tablespoons olive oil, divided
1   zucchini, thinly sliced in
      rounds
1/2   large eggplant, thinly sliced
      lengthwise
1/2   medium red onion, sliced into
      1/2-inch rings
1/2   pound fresh leaf spinach
1   cup half-and-half
2   tablespoons whipping cream
3   tablespoons freshly grated
      Parmesan cheese
      Salt and freshly ground black
      pepper to taste

Cook pasta in large pot of boiling water until al dente; drain and set aside. Dust veal and shrimp with flour. Heat 2 tablespoons oil in large nonstick skillet; sauté veal and shrimp separately. Set aside.

Heat 2 tablespoons oil in same skillet; sauté zucchini and eggplant. Set aside. Heat remaining 1 tablespoon oil in same skillet; sauté onion and spinach 7 minutes.

Toss pasta with veal, shrimp, zucchini, eggplant, onion and spinach. Warm half-and-half, cream and Parmesan; toss with pasta mixture. Heat to serving temperature. Season with salt and pepper.

Serves 4.

 Reduce oil to 3 tablespoons and half-and-half to 1/2 cup.

 White: Dunnewood Chardonnay; Puligny-Montrachet Laboure-Roi (France); Martin Ray Chardonnay.

Red: Beaujolais-Villages Duboeuf (France); Clos Pegase Merlot; Chateau Vieux Telegraphe (France); Barolo Conterno (Italy).

SCALLOPINI DI POLLO

4   boneless, skinless chicken
    breast halves, flattened
    All-purpose flour
6   tablespoons butter
6   ounces mushrooms, sliced
2   teaspoons capers
6   ounces bacon, cooked crisp
4   canned artichoke hearts,
    drained
3   ounces dry white wine
1   tablespoon fresh lemon juice
    Salt and freshly ground black
    pepper to taste

Dust chicken with flour on both sides. Heat butter in large skillet; sauté chicken 5 minutes per side. Add mushrooms and capers; cook 4 minutes. Add bacon, artichokes, wine and lemon juice. Cook over medium-low heat 5 minutes. Season with salt and pepper.

Serves 2.

To lower the fat, limit butter to 2 tablespoons and eliminate bacon.

Ferrari-Carano Fume-Blanc; Bernardus Chardonnay; Mer & Soliel Chardonnay; Chateau Haut-Brion Blanc (France).

CHILLED LEEK SOUP
SAUTE OF CHANTERELLE MUSHROOMS WITH CORN
STEAMED STRIPED BASS
with Wilted Spinach, Sweet Pepper and Lime Sauce
FIGS AND BERRIES
with Key Lime Sorbet and Sabayon

Chez Nous consistently ranks as one of the top restaurants in its category in the United States, so it's not surprising that many food critics say that the best French food in Houston is found in Humble. Some devoted fans have regularly driven a hundred miles or more to have dinner there since it opened in 1984.

Chef/owner Gerard Brach, who is from Alsace, says the right side of his menu is "written in stone," but the left side is subject to whim — his mood, the arrival of some fine foodstuff or a seasonal specialty such as fiddlehead fern. The right side features classics such as Steak Marchand du Vin, escargot, Coquille St. Jacques and Chartreuse of Pheasant. The left side breaks new ground with Normandy Duck Mousse With Plum Wine and Pickled Cherries, Fresh Foie Gras With Caramelized Apples and Honey Vinegar and Mesquite Grilled Rib Eye With Jalapeno Herb Butter.

One salad alone is worth the drive: radicchio and field greens are sandwiched between two squares of crisp-fried won ton skins, which have been slathered on one side with creamy goat cheese mixed with a little sour cream and fresh herbs. The salad is garnished with hearts of palm, radicchio, tomato wedges, cucumbers and red bell pepper. Rack of lamb is such a popular signature dish that Brach sells about 5,000 a year — he only uses lamb raised in New Zealand to his specifications. Duck also calls forth Brach's creative juices — the breast might be roasted and served with a citrus glaze or used in confit, terrines and pate; the carcass goes into stock for onion soup.

Brach, who has encouraged local residents to grow tomatoes and other specialty vegetables for him, now has his own garden. He and his wife, Sandra, transformed a former Pentecostal church into a charming French farm cottage with blue wainscoting, lace curtains, paintings, photographs and touches of copper and dusty rose. Two private rooms are available for small parties, week nights only. Because it is so small, reservations are a must; make them as far ahead as possible for weekends.

Chez Nous has received the DiRona award for distinguished restaurants of North America and the Best of the Best Five Star Diamond Award from the National Academy of Restaurants and Hospitality Sciences among other honors. The 1994/95 Zagat Survey for Houston restaurants gave Chez Nous the top food and top French food rankings.

LITE FARE

French Mediterranean cuisine combines lean meats and seafood with rich and tasty sauces, which can be enjoyed in moderation. Fish selections are mainly northern varieties, halibut and salmon, high in omega-3 fats that may lower cholesterol. This small, quaint restaurant offers personalized service, so special requests are taken seriously.

Chez Nous
217 S. Ave. G
Humble, Tx 77338
446-6717

CHILLED LEEK SOUP

2	leeks, white part only
1/4	cup (1/2 stick) unsalted butter
1	medium-size sweet onion (such as Texas 1015), chopped
2	garlic cloves, chopped
2	cups chicken stock
1	cup whipping cream
1/4	bunch fresh mint, chopped
	Salt and freshly ground black pepper to taste
4	whole basil leaves fried in oil (optional)

Sauté leeks in butter over medium heat in a 1-quart saucepan until soft. Add onion and garlic; cook 3 minutes. Add stock; simmer 12 minutes. Whisk in cream and mint; cook to reduce by half. Puree in blender. Season with salt and pepper; strain through a fine sieve. Chill about 3 to 4 hours.

To serve, ladle chilled soup into cold soup plates and garnish with fried basil leaves.

At the restaurant, the soup is topped with a fried lotus basket filled with Sauvignon Blanc Sorbet

Serves 4.

Reduce butter to 2 tablespoons for sautéing. Substitute evaporated skim milk for cream. Use salt-free, defatted chicken stock.

Enjoy without wine.

SAUTÉ OF CHANTERELLE MUSHROOMS WITH CORN

3	ears corn
1	tablespoon minced shallots
3	tablespoons chopped onion
1	tablespoon each: extra-virgin olive oil and butter
2	ounces applewood bacon, cut in julienne strips
6	ounces cleaned fresh chanterelle or shiitake mushrooms
1/2	cup whipping cream
2	tablespoons chopped fresh basil
1	tablespoon chopped fresh parsley
1	tablespoon fresh lemon juice
	Salt and freshly ground black pepper to taste
4	sprigs fresh thyme

Remove husks and silks from corn. Cook in boiling salted water 4 minutes. Drain and cut kernels from cob; reserve.

Sauté shallots and onion in oil and butter over medium heat in a 1 1/2-quart saucepan until transparent. Add bacon and mushrooms; cook 2 minutes, tossing while cooking. Add corn kernels and cream; simmer until slightly thickened. Add basil, parsley, lemon juice, salt and pepper. Divide among 4 ramekins and garnish each with a sprig of thyme.

Serves 4.

Eliminate butter and oil. Sauté onion and shallots in nonstick pan using nonstick spray. Substitute evaporated skim milk for cream.

Cotes-du-Rhone Guigal (France); Zaca Mesa Pinot Noir Reserve; Rex Hill or Ponzi Pinot Noir Reserve (Oregon)

STEAMED STRIPED BASS
with Wilted Spinach, Sweet Pepper and Lime

4   (7-ounce) bass or halibut or snapper fillets, skin left on
3   tablespoons butter, divided
1   minced shallot
    Sweet Pepper and Lime Sauce (recipe follows)
1   pound spinach, cleaned and stemmed
    Salt and freshly ground black pepper to taste
1   garlic clove, poached and julienned
1   tablespoon each, finely diced: lemon and orange rinds
1   tablespoon chopped chives

SWEET PEPPER AND LIME SAUCE

1   tablespoon butter
1   minced shallot
2   medium-size red bell peppers, seeded and chopped in chunks
1   cup vegetable stock
    Juice of 1 lime
6   tablespoons sweet butter
1/3 bunch chopped cilantro leaves
    Salt and freshly ground black pepper to taste

Preheat oven to 400 degrees. Place fillets in a buttered 2-quart baking dish. Brush fillets with 2 tablespoons butter and sprinkle with shallot; cover tightly with foil and steam in oven until just done (opaque), about 14 minutes.

While fish is baking, prepare Sweet Pepper and Lime Sauce.

Blanch spinach leaves in boiling salted water about 2 minutes; drain well on paper towels. Toss with remaining 1 tablespoon butter, salt and pepper.

To serve, pour a pool of Sweet Pepper and Lime Sauce in center of each warm plate. Place a bed of spinach on top of sauce. Top with fish, skin side up, and sprinkle with garlic, lemon and orange rinds and chives.

Serving Suggestion: Serve with green lima beans and mashed potatoes; garnish with fiddlehead fern.

Sweet Pepper and Lime Sauce

Melt butter in an 8-inch skillet; sauté shallot until transparent. Add red pepper and stock; cook until peppers are tender. Puree in food processor or blender; return to pan and add lime juice. Whisk in butter, a little at a time, swirling constantly. Add cilantro, salt and pepper. Keep warm over hot water.

Serves 4.

Spray baking dish with nonstick spray instead of using butter. Eliminate butter for tossing spinach. Reduce butter to 4 tablespoons in Sweet Pepper and Lime Sauce. Use salt-free vegetable stock.

Meridian Chardonnay; Ferrari-Carano Chardonnay; Far Niente Chardonnay.

FIGS AND BERRIES *with Key Lime Sorbet and Sabayon*

Key Lime Sorbet (recipe
follows)
Sabayon (recipe follows)
8   fresh Mission figs (1 1/4 to
     1 1/2-inch diameter), stemmed
     and halved
1   cup each: fresh raspberries and
     blackberries
1/2 cup fresh red or black currants,
     stemmed
4   shortbread or sugar cookies
4   sprigs fresh mint

Prepare Key Lime Sorbet. Prepare Sabayon. Preheat broiler. Place figs, cut side up, around the inside rim of ovenproof serving plate. Sprinkle with half the berries and currants, spoon Sabayon over fruits and brown under broiler. Sprinkle with remaining fruits. Place a cookie of choice in center of plate and mound a scoop of Key Lime Sorbet on top. Decorate with mint sprig.

KEY LIME SORBET
1/2 cup sugar
3/4 cup water
4   tablespoons key lime juice
4   tablespoons key lime zest (see
     Special Helps section)

SABAYON
3   egg yolks
3   tablespoons sugar
6   tablespoons sauternes
1/4 cup whipping cream, whipped

Key Lime Sorbet

Combine sugar, water, lime juice and zest in a 1-quart saucepan over medium heat. Bring to a boil, reduce to a simmer and cook 5 minutes. Cover and let stand until syrupy, about an hour. Strain, chill and freeze in an ice cream machine. Keep in freezer until needed.

Sabayon

Combine yolks, sugar and wine in a stainless steel mixing bowl. Whisk with a wire whip or hand mixer over a hot water bath until thick and doubled in volume. Whisk over ice until cool. Fold in whipped cream.

Serves 4.

Great way to enjoy a low-fat dessert filled with healthy fresh fruits.

If served without the sorbet — Ferrari-Carano Eldorado Gold (1/2 Bottle); Tokaji Royal Tokaji Wine Company 5 Puttonyos (Hungary); Chateau Climens or Chateau Lafaurie-Peyreguay (France).

SHRIMP DAMIAN
LAMB CHOPS ARNO
POLLO MENICHINO
FEDILINI BUONGUSTAIO

From the time you lay eyes on the mouth-watering array of dishes displayed on the antique antipasto table at the entry of Damian's, you know you can expect a singular fine-dining experience. The restaurant, named for Damian Mandola, who opened it in 1983, was bought by Mandola's cousins, Frank B. Mandola and Joseph "Bubba" Butera in 1993, but still offers the food and wines that quickly earned it a reputation as one of Houston's top Italian restaurants.

The menu, in the capable hands of executive chef Luigi Ferre, gives diners a broad taste of the best of Italy — from the specialties of the Piedmont and Rome to Fiorenza and Tuscany. Ferre visits Italy regularly to refresh the menu and bring back to Houston the best examples of regional cooking. Ferre considers Damian Mandola his mentor and follows his basic philosophy: Use high-quality, fresh food and prepare it simply — "not too much sauce, not too much garlic, not too much decoration," he says.

A popular new addition is a prix fixe, five-course dinner at La Piccola Table di Luigi, a small, glass-enclosed dining area with a view of the kitchen. An expanded banquet room upstairs, which accommodates 120, is the frequent setting for corporate and business entertaining, surprise parties and wedding rehearsal and anniversary dinners.

The low-ceilinged arched dining room looks up to window boxes of flowers at street level. Its muted terra cotta walls, rustic antiques, paintings and framed family photographs, wooden tables with starched white linens and fresh flowers create a warm, friendly setting. At one end is a mural of a pastoral Tuscan scene by artist Joan Loewthal.

Damian's signature dishes include Shrimp Damian, Eggplant Rollatini, Costolette di Maiale Albanese (a marinated pork loin chop grilled and served with caramelized onions, pinenuts and raisins), Involtini di Pollo (chicken breast stuffed with Italian sausage and spinach in a marsala sauce) and Snapper Nino Jr., named for one of Damian Mandola's brothers. A dessert display reminds diners to save room for Damian's specialties — tiramisu, lemon and raspberry tarts and one of Ferre's recent creations, a combination of zabaglione whipped with mascarpone cheese and layered with fresh berries.

--- *LITE FARE* ---

Italian fare is great for healthy dining with an emphasis on carbohydrates in pastas and breads, combined with moderate portions of lean meats, and accompanied with low-fat sauces such as marinara and pomodoro. Dressings and sauces can be served on the side. Vegetables and fish can be grilled or steamed. Special requests are acceptable.

Damian's
3011 Smith St.
Houston, Tx 77006
522-0439

SHRIMP DAMIAN

1/2	cup (1 stick) clarified butter Salt and freshly ground black pepper to taste, divided
28	large shrimp (16/20 count), peeled, deveined, tails on
4	teaspoons each, chopped: garlic and shallots
1	teaspoon lemon zest
1/2	cup each: fish or chicken stock and dry white wine
2	teaspoons fresh lemon juice
3/4	cup (1 1/2 sticks) cold butter
2	teaspoons chopped fresh Italian parsley

Heat clarified butter in skillet over high heat. Salt and pepper shrimp; sauté in butter until shrimp turn pink, about 1 minute. Add garlic, shallots and zest; sauté 2 to 3 minutes. Add stock, wine and lemon juice; cook 1 minute to reduce. Add cold butter, parsley, salt and pepper whisking constantly until smooth and thickened. When sauce is creamy, remove from heat and pour over shrimp.

Serves 4.

Reduce clarified butter to 2 tablespoons for sauteing. Eliminate butter in sauce. Serve with rice or other nonfat starch.

Fetzer Sundial Chardonnay; Silverado Chardonnay; Chablis Raveneau (France); Corton-Charlemagne Louis Latour (France).

LAMB CHOPS ARNO

8	center-cut lamb chops Salt and freshly cracked black pepper to taste
2	tablespoons olive oil
1	teaspoon each: minced garlic and anchovy paste
1	tablespoon chopped fresh rosemary
2	cups dry red wine Dash of balsamic vinegar
2	tablespoons cold butter

Preheat oven to 400 degrees. Season chops with salt and pepper. Heat oil in a large skillet; brown chops rapidly, about 2 to 3 minutes on per side.

Remove chops to baking pan; bake 5 minutes. Meanwhile, add garlic, anchovy paste and rosemary to skillet; cook and stir 1 minute. Deglaze pan (see Special Helps section) with wine and vinegar, scraping up all pan drippings.

Remove chops from oven (should be cooked medium-rare) and return to skillet. Add butter and melt. Remove chops to plate; reduce sauce further if necessary to thicken. Correct salt and pepper seasoning. Pour sauce over chops to serve.

Serves 4.

Cut oil to 1 tablespoon for sauteing. Eliminate butter.

Chateau Meyney (France); Ridge Lytton Springs or Geyserville Zinfandel; Dalla Valle Cabernet Sauvignon or Maya; Chateau Margaux (France).

POLLO MENICHINO

Chicken Marinade (recipe follows)
4   (7- to 8- ounce) whole boneless chicken breasts, halved
6   ounces soft goat cheese (such as Montrachet), divided
2   teaspoons chopped shallot
2   teaspoons crushed fresh lemon thyme leaves
1   cup each: white wine and chicken stock
1/2 cup (1 stick) plus 2 tablespoons chilled butter
    Salt and freshly ground black pepper to taste
4   tablespoons sun-dried tomato slices in oil, drained and julienned

CHICKEN MARINADE
2   garlic cloves, lightly crushed
1   tablespoon chopped fresh lemon thyme leaves
2   tablespoons each: balsamic vinegar and extra-virgin olive oil
1/2 teaspoon salt
1/4 teaspoon freshly ground black pepper

Prepare Chicken Marinade. Add chicken; marinate, covered, in refrigerator 1 to 3 hours. Remove from marinade and grill over charcoal 3 to 4 minutes each side.

Divide cheese into quarters; form each into a small patty. Just before chicken is done, place one round of cheese on each chicken breast to warm up (cheese should not melt completely).

While chicken is grilling, place shallot, thyme, wine and stock in a small skillet. Cook over medium heat to reduce until all but 2 tablespoons remain. Add butter, salt, pepper and tomato. When butter is melted and sauce is creamy, remove chicken from grill, arrange on plate and pour sauce over it.

Note: Be careful with salt because sun-dried tomatoes and goat cheese are very salty.

Serving Suggestion: Serve with pasta and sauteed mixed vegetables.

Chicken Marinade
Combine garlic, thyme, vinegar, oil, salt and pepper in a medium bowl.

Serves 4.

Reduce goat cheese to 4 ounces to make smaller patties. Use salt-free, defatted chicken stock. Eliminate butter in sauce.

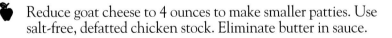

White: Vinho Verde Quinta da Pedra Alvarino (Portugal); Llano Estacado Chardonnay Cellar Select (Texas); Robert Mondavi Chardonnay Reserve.

Red: Fall Creek Granite Reserve (Texas); Llano Estacado Cabernet Sauvignon Cellar Select (Texas); Lewis Cellars or Paul Hobbs Cabernet Sauvignon.

FEDILINI BUONGUSTAIO

4	(4- to 6-ounce) lobster tails (Damian's uses Australian)
1/2	cup (1 stick) clarified butter
4	teaspoons chopped garlic
1	teaspoon each: crushed dried oregano and red pepper flakes
3/4	cup chicken or fish stock (see Special Helps section)
2	cups Pomodoro Sauce (recipe follows)
1	cup Cream Sauce Base (recipe follows)
10	ounces lump crabmeat, cleaned and picked over
12	ounces dry fedilini pasta, cooked

POMODORO SAUCE

4	pounds medium-size Roma tomatoes, cut in quarters (not peeled)
1	red onion, finely chopped
4	garlic cloves, finely chopped
1/4	cup olive oil
1	teaspoon salt
	Pinch each: sugar and freshly ground black pepper
1	small whole carrot, peeled
	Pinch coarsely chopped fresh basil leaves

CREAM SAUCE BASE

1	tablespoon unsalted butter
3/4	cup whipping cream
	Pinch each: kosher salt and ground white pepper

Split lobster tails in half lengthwise; remove meat from shell. Heat butter in a large skillet over medium heat. Place lobster meat and shell in skillet; sauté 3 minutes, turning periodically. Do not overcook. Set lobster aside and keep warm.

Add garlic, oregano and pepper flakes to same skillet; sauté 2 minutes. Add stock; cook until reduced to 1/2 cup. Whisk in Pomodoro Sauce and Cream Sauce Base; cook 3 minutes until reduced to a nice sauce consistency.

Add crabmeat; toss just to warm (do not break crabmeat into small pieces). Add pasta; toss with crab and sauce. Divide pasta among four (10-inch) plates; garnish each with 1 lobster tail and shell.

Pomodoro Sauce

Place tomatoes in a 3-quart saucepan over medium heat. Cook, stirring and mashing until they are soft, about 30 minutes. Put tomatoes through a food mill twice to puree.

In same saucepan, combine onion, garlic and oil. Sauté over medium heat until onion and garlic are soft. Add tomato puree, salt, sugar, pepper and carrot. Bring to a boil; reduce heat and simmer 30 to 45 minutes. Stir frequently, skimming off foam. Taste and adjust seasoning. Turn off heat, remove carrot, add basil and stir. Makes about 1 quart. Will keep one week in refrigerator. Can be used with pasta, fish, mussels or other seafood.

Cream Sauce Base

Melt butter in a small saucepan. Whisk in cream, salt and pepper. Slowly bring to a boil, stirring occasionally. When sauce comes just to a boil, turn off heat. Makes 1 cup.

Serves 4.

🍎 Reduce butter to 1/4 cup for sauteing. Use salt-free, defatted chicken stock. Substitute evaporated skim milk for cream in Cream Sauce Base.

🍇 SIMI Sauvignon-Blanc; Rothbury Estate Chardonnay (Australia); Cloudy Bay Sauvignon-Blanc (New Zealand); Seavey or Sonoma-Cutrer Les Pierres Chardonnay.

PAN-SEARED PORK TENDERLOIN
with Macadamia Nut Chutney and Granny Smith Vinaigrette
CORNFLAKE CINNAMON RAISIN TOAST
ADAM'S MARK BREAD PUDDING
with Kentucky Bourbon Whiskey Sauce

Deco, the showplace restaurant at the Adam's Mark Hotel, has extended Houston's fine dining horizons, and those who venture outside the Loop are rewarded with some of the best food in the city from quick, casual lunches to special-occasion dinners. Recently renovated, the Adam's Mark offers various accommodations for meetings, conventions, weddings, social events, gourmet dining or a night on the town with live entertainment.

Award-winning executive chef Jean-Michel Matos apprenticed with master chef Jacques Maxima in France, has trained with two other master chefs and worked in several four- and five-star hotels. Matos' Progressive Contemporary cooking is mindful of tradition, but stays abreast of the trends. He uses fresh ingredients including herbs from the hotel's carefully tended herb garden. As the hotel's full-service restaurant, Deco serves breakfast, lunch and dinner. Even guests who wish to dine in their rooms can pamper themselves by ordering from the Deco menu. The lunch menu offers burgers, sandwiches, soups, pasta and salads with Thai, Italian, Southwestern, Mediterranean and American regional accents.

Matos oversees the preparation of everything from breakfast to food for 5,000 at any one meal period as well as weekday lunch buffets, an extensive Sunday brunch and weekend seafood and international buffets. Desserts are an awesome temptation. His menus also include health-conscious dishes, and he creates special menus for private parties. The wine list contains more than 200 labels, and many wines are available by the glass.

Mirrored columns topped with wrought iron and beveled glass panels, touches of brown marble, gunmetal green and gold leaf reinforce the restaurant's art deco theme. The distinctive Deco logo is repeated throughout the emerald-green carpeted dining areas, a glass-enclosed private dining area and on wine glasses and specially designed china.

Several of Matos' award-winning signature dishes are the menu mainstays including Roasted Caramelized Duck with Vanilla Bean Jus Over Red and Green Cabbage. Among outstanding appetizers are gnocchi with Roquefort cream and walnuts and sauteed sea scallops in tequila lime marmalade. Entrees include several prime beef dishes and grilled sea bass with tropical fruit chutney.

--- *LITE FARE* ---

Chef Matos believes in developing the natural flavors of foods without masking flavors with high-fat sauces. He specializes in fresh seafood and organically grown vegetables and herbs. Almost everything is prepared in-house, even the fresh mozzarella cheese. The menu offers a variety of northern ocean fish high in omega-3 fatty acids.

Deco
Adam's Mark Hotel
2900 Briarpark
Houston, Tx 77042
978-7400

PAN SEARED PORK TENDERLOIN
with Macadamia Nut Chutney and Granny Smith Vinaigrette

Granny Smith Vinaigrette
(recipe on next page)
6   (12-ounce) pork tenderloins
2   eggs
2   (9-ounce) jars Major Grey's
    mango chutney
1   pound unsalted Macadamia
    nuts or as desired, coarsely
    chopped
1   each, medium-size: yellow, red
    and green bell peppers, finely
    diced
1   medium onion, diced, divided
3/4 cup dry plain bread crumbs
1/2 pound diced bacon, divided
1   medium head red cabbage,
    shredded
1/2 cup each: red wine and red
    wine vinegar
1 1/2 cups sugar, divided
6   whole cloves, divided
    Salt and freshly ground black
    pepper to taste
1   medium head green cabbage,
    shredded
1/2 cup each: white wine and white
    wine vinegar
4   tablespoons caraway seeds
6   tablespoons canola oil
1/2 pound Granny Smith apples,
    cut in wedges for garnish
    Toasted macadamia nuts for
    garnish
1/2 bunch chives for garnish

Prepare Granny Smith Vinaigrette. Use a fairly long, sharp knife to cut almost all the way through the tenderloin lengthwise to make a pocket for stuffing. Repeat for each tenderloin.

In medium bowl, combine eggs, chutney, chopped macadamia nuts, bell peppers and half of onion. Gradually add bread crumbs, using just enough to bind mixture. Stuff tenderloin pockets.

In heavy saucepan, sauté half the remaining onion and half the bacon until translucent. Add red cabbage, red wine, red wine vinegar, 1 cup sugar and 3 cloves. Season with salt and pepper. Cook over medium heat until all liquid is evaporated. Set aside.

In heavy saucepan, sauté remaining onion and bacon until translucent. Add green cabbage, white wine, white wine vinegar, remaining 1/2 cup sugar, remaining 3 cloves and caraway seeds. Season with salt and pepper. Cook over medium heat until all liquid is evaporated. Set aside.

Preheat oven to 350 degrees. Heat oil until hot in large nonstick skillet; brown tenderloins on all sides. Place in baking pan; bake about 20 minutes, or until internal temperature reaches 160 degrees. Remove from oven and let rest.

To serve: Place a 3-inch cookie cutter in middle of each plate as a mold. Place half red cabbage and half green cabbage mixtures into cutter; remove cutter. Line plate with 1/4 cup Granny Smith Vinaigrette. Slice tenderloins on an angle and divide among plates, fanning on top of Vinaigrette. Garnish with apple wedges, toasted macadamia nuts and chives.

Serves 8 to 12.

Modifications and wine suggestions follow Granny Smith Vinaigrette recipe.

GRANNY SMITH VINAIGRETTE

6	Granny Smith apples with skins on
1/4	cup finely chopped shallots
1/2	bunch chives, divided
1/2	cup canola oil
3/4	cup apple juice
1	tablespoon sugar
	Salt and freshly ground black pepper to taste
1/4	cup apple cider vinegar
1	medium-size red bell pepper, seeded and diced

Granny Smith Vinaigrette

Preheat oven to 350 degrees. Place apples in 11x7x2-inch baking dish; roast until tender, about 30 minutes. Or core apples and microwave on high power until tender, about 10 minutes. Let apples cool; core and cut into chunks. In food processor, puree apples, shallots and half of chives. Slowly add oil, apple juice, sugar, salt and pepper. Transfer to a bowl; stir in vinegar, red pepper and remaining chives, finely chopped. Chill, covered; 1 hour. Serve with Pan Seared Pork Tenderloin.

 Reduce: macadamia nuts to 1/2 pound, bacon to 1/4 pound and oil for sauteing tenderloins to 3 tablespoons. Makes 12 servings.

 White: Chateau Ste. Michelle Dry Riesling (Washington); Ockfener Bockstein Riesling Kabinett (Germany); Berncasteler Lay Riesling Kabinett (Germany). Red: Topolos or Elyse Wine Cellars Zinfandel; Kline or DeLoach Zinfandel; Rabbit Ridge or Robert Mondavi Zinfandel.

CORNFLAKE CINNAMON RAISIN TOAST

4	eggs
2	tablespoons sugar
1/2	teaspoon ground cinnamon
1	cup whipping cream
2	cups cornflakes
6	thick slices cinnamon raisin bread
6	tablespoons butter, divided
	Powdered sugar, warm syrup or warm preserves for topping

Combine eggs, sugar, cinnamon and cream in a medium bowl; mix well. Dip a slice of bread into egg mixture; let soak until bread is very moist. Dip bread in cornflakes, making sure all sides are coated with flakes. Repeat with remaining slices.

Melt 3 tablespoons butter in large skillet; add 3 slices bread and cook slowly, about 4 to 5 minutes, turning bread over until both sides are golden brown. Repeat with remaining butter and bread. Cut each slice into triangles; serve with powdered sugar, syrup or preserves.

Serves 6.

 Substitute 4 egg whites and 2 whole eggs for 4 whole eggs and low-fat milk for cream. Eliminate butter and brown in a nonstick skillet using nonstick spray.

 Coffee (regular or decaf) or milk.

ADAM'S MARK BREAD PUDDING
with *Kentucky Bourbon Whiskey Sauce*

4	cups milk
1	cup sugar
8	eggs
1	(1-pound) loaf stale French bread or 6 (2.5-ounce) day-old croissants, sliced thin
	Butter
	Sugar
	Bourbon Whiskey Sauce (recipe follows)

Preheat oven to 325 degrees. Combine milk, sugar and eggs in a medium bowl. Soak bread or croissants in mixture until all pieces are soft. Butter a (9x1 1/2-inch) round or square pan and sprinkle a little sugar over the bottom. Spoon mixture into pan. Set pan in water bath (a larger pan of hot water that comes to within 1/2-inch of top of baking pan). Bake about 45 minutes, until golden brown or knife inserted in center comes out clean. Serve with Bourbon Whiskey Sauce.

BOURBON WHISKEY SAUCE

2	cups whipping cream
3/4	cup (1 1/2 sticks) unsalted butter, softened
1	pound (4 cups) powdered sugar
2	eggs
	Bourbon to taste

Bourbon Whiskey Sauce

In a 2-quart saucepan, whisk together cream, butter and sugar. Stirring frequently, bring mixture to just under a boil, (about 180 degrees on a candy thermometer).

In separate bowl, beat eggs and a little hot cream together to temper eggs to prevent curdling. Add mixture to saucepan, whisking constantly. Cook 2 minutes; do not let boil. Remove from heat and whisk in bourbon.

Serves 8.

🍎 Enjoy a small portion and balance with a low-fat meal.

🍇 How about a shot of Kentucky Bourbon Whiskey!

FACING PAGE, FROM LEFT: John Sheely, Riviera Grill; Jim Mills, The Houstonian; Douglas Bass, The Brownstone.

FOLLOWING PAGE, FROM LEFT: Tony Ruppe, DeVille; Joe Mannke, Rotisserie for Beef and Bird; Scott Chen, Empress; Gerard Brach, Chez Nous.

PENNE PASTA WITH SAUTEED CHICKEN
and Spinach Cream Sauce
GRILLED BEEF TENDERLOIN ON POTATO-THYME CAKE
with Chipotle Cream
CARPACCIO OF BEEFSTEAK TOMATOES WITH SPINACH, ARUGULA AND BALSAMIC VINAIGRETTE
PUMPKIN CREAM BRULE WITH FRESH BERRY COMPOTE

DeVille, the award-winning restaurant at the Four Seasons Hotel, is one of the standard-setters that have elevated fine dining in Houston and brought national acclaim to our chefs. Executive chef Tony Ruppe worked his way up in his profession through Brennan's, the Royal Sonesta and Hyatt Regency hotels in New Orleans and served an apprenticeship in Switzerland before he came to Houston in 1985 as executive sous chef of the former Remington Hotel (now the Ritz-Carlton). Recently he has been a guest chef at the Regent Hotel in Bangkok, an Aspen Food and Wine Festival event and the James Beard House in New York City as part of the Best Hotel Chefs series. He is a driving force in the local Share Our Strength benefit and other anti-hunger projects.

Ruppe takes a hands-on approach: salmon, chicken, bacon and prosciutto are smoked on-site along with pancetta (uncured Italian bacon), and all meats are hand-cut. Sausages, wine vinegars, jams, jellies, relishes, sauces, pickles, pestos, infused oils, breads, ice creams, sorbets, candies and other desserts also are made in the hotel kitchens. Menus feature fresh seasonal specialties from salmon from the Pacific Northwest to exotic mushrooms from the East Coast. Ruppe is particularly interested in Thai and other Asian cooking.

The restaurant has received the DiRona Award, the Wine Spectator's Award of Excellence and the Zagat Survey's 1994/95 Houston restaurants' highest rating for Best New American Cuisine, Best Sunday Brunch and Best Hotel Dining. The hotel holds the Mobil Four-Star Award and in 1995 received the Triple A's coveted Five-Diamond award.

Ruppe, who oversees all menu planning and food preparation for DeVille, Terrace Cafe and Lobby Lounge, catered events and room service, has observed that today's guests are more health-conscious. The hotel's Alternative Cuisine menu has gained in popularity and the chef recently added a vegetarian category to the menu. Guests and social movers and shakers who come for business meetings, celebratory occasions, entertaining special guests and indulgent dining describe the food in superlatives. Even the salads are memorable.

DeVille, with its rotating art exhibits and elegant, but restful, decor, overlooks the George R. Brown Convention Center downtown. The hotel also offers a dinner-and-the-theater evening of leisurely dining, and the downtown trolley delivers you to the door of any Theater District theater.

--- *LITE FARE* ---

The DeVille menu features Alternative Cuisine that is nutritionally balanced and lower in calories, cholesterol and fat. Executive Chef Tony Ruppe has designed menu items that balance lean, smaller portions (less than 6 ounces) of fish with grains and vegetables. Several Vegetarian items are also marked. Enjoy an array of complex carbohydrates.

DeVille
Four Seasons Hotel
1300 Lamar
Houston, Tx 77010
650-1300

PENNE PASTA WITH SAUTEED CHICKEN
and Spinach Cream Sauce

2   tablespoons olive oil
2   (6-ounce) skinless, boneless chicken breasts, cut into strips
1   cup quartered mushrooms
4   garlic cloves, minced
1/4 cup chardonnay
1   cup spinach, stemmed, washed, blanched in boiling water and chopped
3   cups dry penne pasta, cooked, drained and cooled
2   tablespoons butter
1/2 cup freshly grated Parmesan cheese, divided
    Salt and freshly ground black pepper to taste

Make Spinach Cream Sauce; set aside. Heat oil in heavy skillet over high heat; sauté chicken. Reduce heat to medium high; add mushrooms and garlic. Cook until mushrooms are done. Add chardonnay and spinach; mix well. Stir in Spinach Cream Sauce and pasta; mix well. Swirl in butter and 1/4 cup cheese. Season with salt and pepper. Serve in warm pasta bowls; top with remaining 1/4 cup cheese.

SPINACH CREAM SAUCE

2   tablespoons olive oil
2   garlic cloves, minced
1   shallot, minced
1/2 cup chicken stock
1/4 cup chardonnay
3/4 cup whipping cream
1   cup spinach that has been stemmed, washed, blanched in boiling water, drained and chopped
1   tablespoon chopped fresh Italian parsley
    Salt and freshly ground black pepper to taste

Spinach Cream Sauce

Heat oil in Teflon-coated skillet; sauté garlic and shallot until translucent. Add stock and wine; simmer until reduced by half. Add cream; simmer until reduced by half. Stir in spinach and parsley; cook about 5 minutes. Season with salt and pepper. Puree in blender; strain through sieve. May be made as long as 1 hour before serving.

Serves 4.

🍎 Use just 1 tablespoon oil to sauté chicken. Eliminate butter and reduce Parmesan cheese to 1/4 cup. Use salt-free, defatted chicken stock. Substitute half-and-half for cream.

🍇 Orvieto Castello della Sala (Italy); Pinot Grigio Collavini (Italy); any Chablis Grand Cru (France).

GRILLED BEEF TENDERLOIN ON POTATO-THYME CAKE
with Chipotle Cream

1   ear corn
     Chipotle Cream (recipe
     follows)
     Potato-Thyme Cake (recipe
     follows)
4   (6-ounce) beef tenderloins
2   tablespoons olive oil
     Salt and freshly ground black
     pepper to taste
1   cup each: spinach and arugula,
     stemmed, washed, spun dry
1/4 cup goat cheese
4   tablespoons sun-dried
     tomatoes, cut into strips and
     slightly rehydrated

CHIPOTLE CREAM

1   tablespoon olive oil
2   garlic cloves, minced
1   shallot, minced
1/4 cup chardonnay
     Juice of 1/2 lime
1   chipotle chile (from a 7-ounce
     can of chipotles in adobo sauce)
1/4 teaspoon sugar
3/4 cup whipping cream
     Salt and freshly ground black
     pepper to taste

POTATO-THYME CAKES

2   Yukon Gold potatoes, peeled
     and grated
1   teaspoon minced fresh thyme
     or to taste
1/2 teaspoon minced fresh Italian
     parsley or to taste
     Salt and freshly ground black
     pepper to taste
4   tablespoons olive oil, divided

Soak corn in salted watr about 10 minutes. Preheat oven to 350 degrees; roast corn in husk 30 minutes. Cool, remove husk and silk; cut corn kernels from cob; reserve. Prepare Chipotle Cream and Potato-Thyme Cakes; reserve.

Coat beef lightly with a little oil; season with salt and pepper. Grill to desired doneness. While beef cooks, heat oil in nonstick skillet over medium heat; sauté spinach and arugula until wilted. Season with salt and pepper; set aside. Repeat above procedure to sauté corn kernels; set aside.

To serve: Place potato cake in center of plate; arrange spinach and arugula on top of cake. Drizzle Chipotle Cream around potato cake; sprinkle corn on Cream. Crumble cheese on Cream; add tomato strips. Place beef on top of spinach and arugula. Serve hot.

Chipotle Cream

Heat oil in small skillet; sauté garlic and shallot until translucent. Add wine, lime juice, chile and sugar; cook to reduce until almost dry. Add cream; cook to reduce until mixture coats the back of a spoon. Puree in blender; do not strain. Season with salt and pepper. May be made as long as 1 hour before serving.

Potato-Thyme Cakes

Mix potatoes, thyme, parsley, salt and pepper in a medium bowl. Heat 1 tablespoon oil in a nonstick skillet over medium heat. Place one-fourth of the potato mixture in skillet; spread out to form a thin cake. Sauté until browned and crisp on one side; turn and brown other side. Repeat with remaining potato mixture and oil. May be made as long as 1/2 hour before serving.

Serves 4.

🍎 Use just 1 tablespoon oil for coating beef. Substitute half-and-half for cream. Cut oil to 2 tablespoons for sauteing Potato-Thyme Cakes.

🍇 Pheasant Ridge Cabernet Sauvignon (Texas) or Warwick Cabernet Sauvignon (South Africa); David Bruce or Ridge York Creek Petite Syrah; Coudoulet de Beaucastel (France).

CARPACCIO OF BEEFSTEAK TOMATOES WITH SPINACH, ARUGULA AND BALSAMIC VINAIGRETTE

1	each, large: yellow and red beefsteak tomatoes Salt and freshly ground black pepper to taste
2	cups each: spinach and arugula, stemmed, washed and blotted dry
6	tablespoons extra-virgin olive oil, divided
5	tablespoons balsamic vinegar, divided
1/2	small red onion, sliced very thin

Select tomatoes that are fully ripe but still firm. Wash and pat dry. Remove core; slice tomatoes paper thin and arrange, alternating yellow and red slices for best color contrast, on large chilled salad plates. Season tomatoes lightly with salt and pepper.

Place spinach and arugula in medium bowl. Drizzle 4 tablespoons oil and 3 tablespoons vinegar over greens. Season with salt and pepper. Toss gently and arrange into high mounds in center of tomatoes. Drizzle remaining 2 tablespoons oil and 2 tablespoons vinegar over tomatoes. Sprinkle sliced onion on top. Serve immediately.

Serves 4.

 Reduce oil to 2 teaspoons.

Beringer White Zinfandel.

PUMPKIN CREAM BRULE WITH FRESH BERRY COMPOTE

6	eggs
1	cup sugar, divided
1	cup canned pumpkin
1/2	vanilla bean or 1/2 teaspoon vanilla
1/4	teaspoon each, ground: cinnamon and nutmeg
1/8	teaspoon ground cloves
2	cups whipping cream
1/2	cup each: fresh raspberries and blackberries
4	sprigs mint for garnish

Preheat oven to 325 degrees. Combine eggs and 1/2 cup sugar in a medium bowl; add pumpkin, mixing well. Cut vanilla bean in half lengthwise; scrape seeds from inside of bean. Add vanilla, cinnamon, nutmeg, cloves and cream; mix well. Strain through sieve. Pour mixture into four (6-ounce) ovenproof or china souffle dishes. Set souffle dishes in water bath (a large pan of hot water that comes to within 1/2-inch of top of souffle dishes). Bake 30 to 45 minutes. When done, remove dishes from water bath and let cool.

Mix berries and 1/4 cup sugar in small bowl; set aside and allow to macerate. Just before serving, sprinkle remaining 1/4 cup sugar evenly over top of each brule. Place under hot broiler, close to heat. Broil just until the sugar begins to caramelize and turn brown. Remove from broiler; briefly cool. Top with berries and a sprig of mint. Serve immediately.

Serves 4.

 Balance a small portion with a low-fat entree.

Commandaria St. John (Cyprus); Hardy's Tall Ships Tawny Port (Australia); Dow Boardroom Port or Croft Distinction Port (Portugal).

BONELESS QUAIL
WITH SHREDDED VEGETABLES FLAMBE
CRISPY CHICKEN
with Lemon Sauce
PEANUTS AND GINGER SOUP
CHOCOLATE BROWNIE FUDGE

Scott Chen, owner/executive chef of Empress restaurant, is the emperor of the unexpected. He incorporates ideas, cooking techniques and ingredients of classic French, Chinese and American cooking to produce new Fusion Cuisine taste sensations: quail is seasoned with ginger, oyster sauce, Chinese pickles and sesame oil, then flambeed over shredded vegetables. Fresh foie gras is grilled and served with an arugula salad with tomatoes in a light vinaigrette.

EMPRESS

Food is paired with compatible wines from a cellar of more than 18,000 bottles representing almost 800 of the world's finest labels. The dessert menu includes more than 20 decadent desserts such as Fresh Mango Creme Brule with mixed sorbets, Tiramisu With Caramel Sauce and Chocolate Walnut Cheesecake. Chen updates stale classics in a fresher, healthier way: Lemon Chicken is done with a light, crispy batter and tart-sweet fresh lemon sauce; stir-fries feature veal with fresh basil or fresh mushrooms with a brown sauce. The expected lychee nuts for dessert come to the table as Dragon Eye Fruits with a stuffing of strawberry cream cheese and strawberry sauce.

After his family immigrated to Houston from Taiwan in 1981, Chen became interested in Chinese cooking while working at a restaurant owned by his sister-in-law. Empress opened in 1985 as the Empress of China. Travel and learning about wines have had a profound influence on his style, which has progressed from Nouvelle Chinese to Pacific Rim to Fusion. Chen is constantly creating new cross-cultural dishes.

His creative dishes have brought him national attention in recent years; he has been invited to be a guest chef at the James Beard House in New York City three times and is included in a "Great Chefs, Great Cities" television series and accompanying cookbook. Empress has won the DiRona and Wine Spectator awards and the Best of the Best designation from the American Academy of Restaurant and Hospitality Sciences.

Chen is expanding the wine cellar and creating a party room for wine- and food-tastings and Gourmet Dinners. His White-Glove Special Fusion Cuisine multi-course dinners attract fine-food lovers from all over the area.

LITE FARE

This Fusion Cuisine restaurant offers innovative and savory dishes for the healthy diner. Chef Scott Chen prepares dishes with little fat using what he describes as "quick saute" cooking. Always on the cutting edge of innovative ideas, Chef Chen believes in developing the natural flavors of foods. Low-sodium soy sauce is used.

Empress
5419-A FM 1960 West
Houston, Tx 77069
583-8021

BONELESS QUAIL WITH SHREDDED VEGETABLES FLAMBE

3   ounces rice wine or white wine
4   tablespoons chopped garlic, divided
1/2 cup Old Vintage Oyster Sauce (available at Asian market)
4   large boneless quail
2   tablespoons extra-virgin olive oil, divided
1/2 each, shredded: carrot and potato
2   tablespoons thinly sliced green onion
1   cup chicken broth
2   tablespoons fresh lemon juice
    Salt to taste
1   green onion stem, sliced
2   tablespoons finely chopped ginger
4   tablespoons chopped Chinese baby cabbage or pickle
1   tablespoon low-sodium soy sauce
1   tablespoon sugar
1   tablespoon each: white wine vinegar and sesame oil
4   fresh basil leaves for garnish
    Rum (optional)

Combine wine, 2 tablespoons garlic and oyster sauce in a medium bowl. Marinate quail in mixture covered in refrigerator 2 to 3 hours. Remove quail from marinade; reserve. Heat 1 tablespoon olive oil in a large skillet; when oil sizzles, sauté quail on each side 4 minutes. Reserve quail.

Sauté carrot, potato and sliced onion in same skillet 2 minutes; add broth, lemon juice and salt; cook 4 minutes. Reserve.

Heat remaining 1 tablespoon olive oil in skillet; add remaining 2 tablespoons garlic, 1 sliced green onion, ginger, cabbage, 2 tablespoons reserved marinade, soy sauce, sugar, vinegar and sesame oil. Cook over medium heat until vegetables are crisp-tender.

Divide sauteed carrot mixture among four plates; place quail on top of each. Top quail with cabbage mixture and garnish with basil leaf. If desired, pour rum over quail and light carefully with a match to flambe. Serve as appetizer or entree.

Serves 4.

🍎 Limit oil to 1 tablespoon, 1/2 tablespoon for sauteing quail and 1/2 tablespoon for vegetables. Use salt-free, defatted chicken stock. Remove skin before eating quail.

🍇 White: Kingston Estate Chardonnay (Australia); Pouilly-Fuisse Louis Latour (France); Blain-Gagnard Chassagne-Montrachet (France).

Red: Beaujolais-Villages Jadot (France); Givry Domaine Joblot (France); Beaune Clos des Ursules or Teurons (France).

CRISPY CHICKEN *with Lemon Sauce*

Lemon Sauce (recipe follows)
3/4 pound boneless, skinless chicken breasts
1/4 teaspoon each: salt and white pepper
1 egg yolk, lightly beaten
6 tablespoons cornstarch, divided
2 tablespoons all-purpose flour
3 cups vegetable oil for deep frying

LEMON SAUCE
1/3 cup each: water and sugar
1/4 cup fresh lemon juice
1/4 teaspoon salt
1 teaspoon cornstarch dissolved in 2 tablespoons water
1 tablespoon olive oil

Prepare Lemon Sauce; reserve. Lay chicken flat on counter; cut diagonally into thin slices. Combine salt, pepper, egg yolk and 1 tablespoon cornstarch in a medium bowl; mix well. Add chicken pieces; stir and marinate 10 minutes. Combine remaining 5 tablespoons cornstarch and flour; dredge chicken in mixture. Heat 3 cups oil in a wok or heavy-bottom deep pan just until it begins to smoke (400 degrees in a deep fryer). Fry chicken about 45 seconds. Drain on paper towels; arrange on serving plate. Pour Lemon Sauce over chicken.

Lemon Sauce

Combine water, sugar, lemon juice and salt in a 1-quart saucepan over medium-high heat. When it comes to a boil, add dissolved cornstarch; whisk until thickened. Whisk in oil to give sauce shine.

Serves 4.

 Balance this delectable chicken dish with plain rice and steamed vegetables.

Sparkling: Friexenet Cordon Negro (Spain); Iron Horse Wedding Cuvee Sparkling Wine: Veuve-Clicquot Ponsardin (France); Krug Rose' (France).

White: Lindeman's Chardonnay Bin 65 (Australia); Pheasant Ridge or Slaughter-Leftwich Chardonnay (Texas); Matanzas Creek or Chateau Montelena Chardonnay.

PEANUTS AND GINGER SOUP

This old Chinese remedy is considered a restorative and is only prepared for family and special friends. It can be served as a dessert.

1/2 fresh ginger root (about 4 ounces)
2 cups water
3/4 pound peeled peanuts (available at Asian market)
3/4 cup brown sugar (not packed)

Clean ginger; peel. Smash ginger until crushed. Pour water into a 2-quart saucepan; bring to a boil. Add ginger; cook 10 minutes. Remove ginger and add peanuts to boiling water; boil 20 minutes. Turn off heat, cover and let stand 10 minutes, then bring to a boil again. Add sugar; mix well and serve in bowls.

Serves 4.

 Peanuts although high in fat are a good source of vitamin E, a desirable antioxidant. Ginger has a reputation in folklore as a medication to settle the stomach.

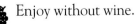 Enjoy without wine.

CHOCOLATE BROWNIE FUDGE

4	cups finely chopped semisweet Swiss chocolate
1 3/4	cups brown sugar (not packed)
2	cups whipping cream
8	egg yolks
2	tablespoons rum compound (available at liquor or gourmet stores)
2	tablespoons all-purpose flour
1/2	cup chopped walnuts
1/3	cup unsalted butter, melted
1/2	cup granulated sugar

Preheat oven to 400 degrees. Combine chocolate, brown sugar and cream in a heavy 3-quart saucepan. Stirring frequently, cook over medium heat until chocolate is melted; cool. Whisk eggs in a large bowl until well beaten. Pour chocolate mixture into eggs, add rum compound and thoroughly combine. Add flour and walnuts; mix well.

Brush butter evenly over bottom and sides of a 12x18x3/4-inch baking pan; pour mixture into pan. Bake on center rack in oven 20 minutes, or until cake tester inserted in center comes out clean. Remove pan from oven; sprinkle granulated sugar evenly over top of brownie. Return pan to oven and bake 2 minutes. Remove pan from oven; let stand 10 minutes. Cut into 3x2-inch bars. Serve with fresh fruit or ice cream.

Makes 36 bars.

 Indulge in moderation.

Any Australian Muscat or Liqueur Muscat; Domecq Pedro Ximenez Sherry (Spain); any rich Cabernet Sauvignon. OK, it's not a dessert wine, but try it!

HOUSTON IS COOKING
The Best

GRILLED CORN SOUP
with Avocado Pico de Gallo
YAKITORI SALMON SALAD
with Buckwheat Noodles and Ponzu Dressing
MANGO RICE PUDDING WITH GINGER CANDY CRUST

The Houstonian Hotel, Club & Spa is a study in visual and culinary contrasts. Nestled in a peaceful natural setting just west of the highly trafficked 610 Loop, it presents a contrasting landscape of towering pines and oaks, ravines and wooded walks bordered with manicured flower beds and lawns. It is a luxury hotel whose 32,000 square feet of meeting space attracts corporate and organization executives as well as health- and fitness-minded guests.

Executive chef Jim Mills' cuisine is rooted in natural, fresh healthful foods that often contrast with their sophisticated flavors and presentations. His new menus express the chef's philosophy that food should be as simple and natural as possible, but intriguing in taste and texture. Mills supervises three meals a day, seven days a week in The Cafe, plus hotel room service, the Manor House (a private facility for club members and hotel guests) and 28 party rooms that can accommodate events of varying size.

The tranquil atmosphere extends to The Cafe, where a large trompe l'oeil mural wall offers sophisticated charm contrasting with the opposite wall of floor-to-ceiling windows overlooking a lush green lawn.

A native of Beaumont, Mills developed his style as a hotel chef in St. Louis, then in Dallas where he was chef de cuisine at The Mansion on Turtle Creek under one of the most recognized new American chefs, Dean Fearing. Later as executive chef at Hotel Crescent Court in Dallas he began to receive national attention. He came to Houston in 1994 as corporate executive chef for Birraporetti's restaurant chain before joining the Houstonian in 1995.

The Cafe is open to the public and offers a global sampling: You might order Huevos Rancheros for breakfast, Tikka Chicken Skewers with Mango Sauce for lunch and Yakitori Salmon with Japanese Buckwheat Noodles for dinner. Low-fat dishes include such inventive fare as Grilled Vegetable "steaks" with Tuscan bean salad and lemon-basil pesto; Grilled Veal Paillard on Creamy Mushroom Risotto With Peperonata; and BBQ Seared Chicken Breast on Cajun Macque Choux with Vegetable Slaw.

THE HOUSTONIAN
HOTEL, CLUB & SPA

LITE FARE

Chef Jim Mills has rededicated The Houstonian to healthy dining with designated dishes that are low in fat and calories while high in flavor. Using low-fat and no-fat substitutes, the Houstonian Healthy Dining Program offers everything from Ancho Glazed Shrimp and Corn Tamale to Grilled Vegetable "Steaks." Calories and fat grams are listed.

*The Houstonian
Hotel, Club and Spa
111 N. Post Oak Lane
Houston, Tx 77024
680-2626*

THE HOUSTONIAN

63

GRILLED CORN SOUP *with Avocado Pico de Gallo*

3   ears yellow corn, shucked and silked
1/2 teaspoon canola oil
     Salt and freshly ground black pepper to taste
1   slice smoked bacon, cut crosswise into 3/8-inch strips
1   medium-size red onion, chopped
6   garlic cloves, finely minced
1   bay leaf, crumbled
5   cups defatted chicken stock
3   (8-inch) corn tortillas, cut into thin strips
     Avocado Pico de Gallo (recipe follows)
4   sprigs cilantro

Preheat oven to 350 degrees. Rub corn lightly with oil; season with salt and pepper. Cook on preheated grill over coals that have burned to gray ash. Corn may be broiled if grilling is inconvenient.

Stand each ear of corn on end and remove kernels with a chef's knife. Do not cut too closely as the bases of the kernels are chewy. Reserve kernels and cobs separately.

Place bacon in a soup pot set over medium-high heat. Cook until almost crisp, then discard fat. Add onion to pot and cook until transparent. Add garlic; cook until mixture begins to brown. Add bay leaf and stock; bring to a boil. Add reserved corn cobs, then reduce heat to a simmer and cook 25 minutes.

Place tortilla strips on a sheet pan; spray with nonstick spray. Bake in oven 10 minutes, or until crisped. Remove from oven and drain thoroughly on paper toweling. Reserve for soup garnish.

When broth is cooked, remove cobs with tongs. Add Avocado Pico de Gallo to pot, stir and correct seasoning. Ladle into heated soup bowls; top with tortilla strips and cilantro sprigs. Serve immediately.

AVOCADO PICO DE GALLO

3   Roma tomatoes, peeled, cored and seeded (see note)
1   serrano chile, stem, vein and seeds removed; finely minced
4   tablespoons roughly chopped cilantro leaves
3/4 teaspoon salt
1   teaspoon freshly ground black pepper
1   avocado, cut into 1 1/4-inch pieces
1   tablespoon fresh lime juice

Avocado Pico de Gallo

Dice tomatoes into 3/8-inch cubes; transfer to medium bowl. Add chile, cilantro, salt, pepper, avocado and lime juice; toss well to combine. Set aside.

Note: To prepare, remove the stem core, then cut a shallow "x". Plunge tomatoes into simmering water on long fork or with slotted spoon. When skin begins to pull away from cuts, remove to a cutting board and let stand a few minutes to cool. Then skin should peel off easily with a paring knife. Halve each peeled tomato and squeeze out seeds and juice.

Serves 4.

By eliminating the Avocado Pico de Gallo, the fat can be reduced from 37% to 21%, but avocado is a good fat. Enjoy and cut another "bad" fat from somewhere else.

Fall Creek or Llano Estacado Chenin-Blanc (Texas); Joseph Phelps Gewurztraminer; Niersteiner Pettenthal Riesling Spatlese Anton Balbach (Germany).

YAKITORI SALMON SALAD
with Buckwheat Noodles and Ponzu Dressing

1	pound boneless, skinless salmon fillets
10	ounces buckwheat soba noodles (available at Asian market)
2/3	cup each, finely julienned: carrot and daikon radish
4	scallions, thinly sliced on the diagonal Ponzu Dressing (recipe follows)
4	ounces mizuna greens (or field salad) or curly endive, spinach or red oak leaf lettuce Yakitori Glaze (recipe follows)
1/2	red bell pepper, seeded and finely diced
1	tablespoon lightly toasted sesame seeds (see note)

YAKITORI GLAZE

1/2	cup each: soy sauce or tamari and sake
2	tablespoons honey
1/2	garlic clove, minced

PONZU DRESSING

1/3	cup each: fresh orange, lemon and lime juices
1/4	cup seasoned rice vinegar
2	tablespoons freshly grated ginger
1	teaspoon canola oil
1/2	teaspoon each: dark sesame oil and salt
1/8	teaspoon cayenne pepper

Dice salmon into 3/4-inch cubes. Soak 4 (10- to 12-inch) bamboo skewers in hot water 20 minutes. Thread salmon onto skewers, about 8 pieces per skewer. Cover and refrigerate until needed.

Bring 2 quarts lightly salted water to a boil in large pot. Add noodles; cook until firm but not chewy, about 7 minutes. When cooked, drain and rinse with cold water; drain again. Toss with carrot, daikon, scallions and 1 cup Ponzu Dressing. Set aside. Wash and sort greens; drain well.

Rub grill with oil to reduce sticking. Dip salmon skewers briefly into Yakitori Glaze; drain and place on grill. Cook, basting and turning, until just done, about 3 minutes. Salmon may also be broiled if grilling is inconvenient. When salmon is just done, set aside and keep warm.

To assemble dish, arrange greens on four plates, stems toward center and tips outward. Divide noodle mixture among plates, placing in center of each. Sprinkle with bell pepper and sesame seeds. Remove salmon from skewers; arrange on greens around noodles. Drizzle a bit of Ponzu Dressing around each plate; serve immediately.

Yakitori Glaze
Combine soy sauce, sake, honey and garlic in small bowl. Stir well, cover and set aside in cool place.

Ponzu Dressing
Combine orange, lemon and lime juices, rice vinegar, ginger, canola and sesame oils, salt and cayenne in small bowl. Stir well, cover and set aside in cool place. Makes 1 1/2 cups.

Serves 4.

🍎 Great low-fat recipe! Use low-sodium soy sauce instead of regular.

🍇 White: Fall Creek Emerald Riesling (Texas); Iron Horse Fume-Blanc; Sancerre Dom-Rossignol (France).

Red: Benton Lane Pinot Noir (Oregon); Domaine des Galluches Bourgueil (France); Domaine Drouhin Pinot Noir (Oregon). (You can serve the first two wines slightly chilled.)

MANGO RICE PUDDING WITH GINGER CANDY CRUST

3/4 cup white or brown rice
1/2 cup egg substitute
1 cup evaporated skim milk
1/3 cup honey
1 teaspoon vanilla
   Pinch of salt
1/4 cup golden raisins
1 large mango, peeled, seeded and diced into 1-inch cubes (1 cup)
1 cup low-fat sour cream
2 tablespoons freshly grated ginger
1/2 cup granulated or brown sugar
   Fresh mint sprigs (optional)

Preheat oven to 350 degrees. Cook rice until just done. Spread out on pan to cool. Combine egg substitute, skim milk, honey, vanilla and salt in a medium bowl. Beat well to mix thoroughly, then stir in rice, raisins and mango. Pour into an 8-inch casserole sprayed lightly with nonstick spray. Spread mixture evenly in dish.

Bake 8 minutes; stir. Bake another 8 minutes; stir. Cook a final 8 minutes, remove from oven and stir in sour cream. Spread mixture evenly in dish; let stand until cooled.

Spread grated ginger on surface of pudding, then sprinkle with sugar. Use a preheated broiler to caramelize sugar topping until well browned, 3 to 5 minutes under broiler. Repeat this process with additional sugar for a thicker, crunchier topping. Take care not to touch the sugar as it is extremely hot. The caramel will harden as it cools. Serve within 2 hours.

To serve, place finished pudding before guests and crack candy topping with a spoon as the servings are presented. May be decorated with sprigs of fresh mint, if desired.

Note: Sugar may be caramelized with a propane torch a la Julia Child.

Serves 8.

Excellent recipe using low-fat ingredients.

Harvey's Gold Cap Port (Portugal); Blandy's or Miles Bual or Malmsey Madeira (Portugal); Muscat Rivesaltes Domaine Cazes (France); Chateau Suduiraut or Raymon-Lafon (France).

GAZPACHO EL REY
SMOKED SALMON JULIENNE WITH ENDIVE
ROAST LAMB RACK WITH HERB AND MUSTARD
GRAND MARNIER SOUFFLE

Dining at La Tour d'Argent with its fine food and wines, attentive service and relaxing atmosphere is the culinary equivalent of a weekend getaway. Many consider it the most romantic restaurant in Houston because of its cozy dining nooks and three "proposal" tables. Whenever making the best impression on guests is a priority — for business meetings, private parties, special occasions and wine dinners — La Tour is the perfect choice. To enhance its reputation as one of Houston's premiere French restaurants, owner Sonny Lahham visits Paris several times a year and recently sent chef Hessni Malla there to study trends.

The restaurant on White Oak Bayou evolved from a log cabin built in 1917 and is known as the oldest log cabin in Houston. It was moved to the site but was almost destroyed by fire just before the opening in 1981. Lahham, his wife and several friends scraped and renovated the burned logs, one by one, and the restaurant opened only slightly off schedule.

Lahham has continued his hands-on approach. Other additions were made in 1993 including a new upstairs wine room. Lahham himself built the most recent addition, a beautifully appointed dining room with plank floors, wood-paneled walls and one long window wall that resembles mullioned glass. Dramatic torchiers that graced the former La Hacienda de los Morales line the walls. Still, the building looks almost indigenous to its wooded setting, especially since birds, raccoons, squirrels and other wild life can frequently be spotted from dining rooms on various levels.

Inside more than 2,000 hunting trophies (including tiger skins and rhinoceros heads), stone fireplaces and beamed ceilings accentuate the hunting lodge ambiance. As counterpoint, leaded glass doors and windows, sparkling chandeliers, hand-crafted chairs, master paintings and fine china create a luxurious setting.

Classics such as pate, chateaubriand, filet mignon, escargot and rack of lamb are mainstays of the menu, but it also offers heart-healthy specialties.

Malla trained in Europe before he came to the United States as chef at the Warwick Hotel (now the Wyndham Warwick). He helped open the Westin Galleria, worked at the former Biscayne and owned his own restaurant, the Vendome, in Conroe before joining La Tour d'Argent in 1989.

--- *LITE FARE* ---

The classic French cuisine at La Tour d'Argent features lean meats; veal, fish and chicken, with luscious specialty sauces. To lower fat and sodium, ask for sauces to be served on the side. Daily specials are available that are low in calories, fat and cholesterol. Special requests are encouraged, so ask for your food to be prepared steamed, poached or grilled.

La Tour d'Argent
2011 Ella Blvd.
Houston, Tx 77008
864-9864

GAZPACHO EL REY

5	medium-size ripe tomatoes, peeled, seeded and cut into cubes
2	medium-size green bell peppers, seeded and cut into cubes
1	cucumber, peeled and cut into chunks
1	small yellow onion, cut into chunks
5	teaspoons virgin olive oil
1 1/2	teaspoons fresh lemon juice
1	teaspoon wine vinegar
1/4	teaspoon bottled hot pepper sauce Worcestershire sauce, salt and freshly ground black pepper to taste Shrimp, peeled and deveined or lump crabmeat, cleaned and picked over for garnish

Combine tomatoes, bell pepper, cucumber, onion, oil, lemon juice, vinegar, pepper sauce, Worcestershire, salt and pepper in a medium bowl; puree, then strain. Ladle into individual bowls; garnish with shrimp or crabmeat as desired.

Serves 4.

Reduce oil to 2 teaspoons and enjoy.

Wine: Rioja Blanc Marques de Caceres (Spain); Cotes-du-Rhone Blanc Domaine de la Becassone Andre Brunel (France); Coudoulet de Beaucastel Blanc (France).

SMOKED SALMON JULIENNE WITH ENDIVE

2	whole endive, washed and drained
3	ounces smoked salmon
1	tablespoon sherry vinaigrette dressing
2	radishes, fashioned into roses for garnish
2	lemon twists for garnish Fresh parsley for garnish

Remove 3 leaves from each whole endive; reserve for garnish. Cut remainder of endive into 2-inch pieces. Julienne salmon; pat dry then mix with vinaigrette. Arrange 3 endive leaves on each plate, garnish with radish rose and lemon twist. Place salmon in center.

Serves 2.

Substitute fat-free vinaigrette dressing for regular.

Domaine Ste. Michelle Sparkling Wine (Washington); Roederer Estate Brut Sparkling Wine; Pol Roger or Charles Heidsieck Brut Champagne (France); Louis Roederer Brut Cristal Champagne (France).

ROAST LAMB RACK WITH HERB AND MUSTARD

2 (8-rib) racks of Australian
   lamb, cut in half (about 4
   pounds total)
2 tablespoons unsalted butter,
   divided
2 tablespoons Dijon mustard
1 teaspoon chopped shallot
2 garlic cloves, crushed
1 teaspoon dried rosemary
1/2 cup bread crumbs
1 1/2 teaspoons brandy
3 ounces brown sauce (see
   Special Helps section)

Preheat oven to 350 degrees. Melt 1 tablespoon butter in a large ovenproof skillet or pan; sauté rack (2 sections) of lamb until golden brown. Repeat with remaining 1 tablespoon butter and rack of lamb. Combine mustard, shallot, garlic and rosemary in a small bowl; smear over lamb. Transfer to oven; bake 20 minutes for medium-well done. Sprinkle bread crumbs over top; place under broiler 2 to 3 minutes to brown crumbs.

Note: American lamb is larger; adjust portions if using domestic lamb.

Serves 4.

🍎 Eliminate butter by sauteing lamb in a nonstick skillet using nonstick spray.

🍇 Laurel Glen REDS; Catena Cabernet Sauvignon (Argentina); Silver Oak Alexander Valley or Jordan Cabernet Sauvignon; Grange (Australia).

GRAND MARNIER SOUFFLE

1 cup Pastry Cream (recipe
   follows)
6 egg whites
1/3 cup Grand Marnier, divided
   Powdered sugar

Prepare Pastry Cream day before needed, if possible. Preheat oven to 325 degrees. Beat egg whites until fluffy. Fold Pastry Cream in by hand. Fold in 1/4 cup Grand Marnier. Butter and dust with sugar 2 (8-ounce) souffle cups. Bake 20 minutes, until souffle puffs out and is brown on top. Top with a sprinkling of remaining Grand Marnier and powdered sugar.

PASTRY CREAM

2 cups milk
1 1/2 cups sugar
4 egg yolks
1/2 teaspoon cornstarch

Pastry Cream

Combine milk and sugar in a 2-quart saucepan; bring to a boil. Reduce heat and whisking constantly, add egg yolks. Continue stirring until thickened, about 15 minutes over low heat. Cover and chill until cold, 24 hours if possible.

Serves 2.

🍎 Savor a sensible portion.

🍇 Coteaux du Layon, Quarts de Chaume or Vouvray Moelleux (France); Beerenauslese or Eiswein (Germany) or Sauternes (France); Far Niente Dolce.

SMOKED TOMATO AND SPINACH DIP
SPINACH QUESADILLAS
SALMON CAKES
LEMON CHESS PIE

Restaurateur Bill Sadler is constantly challenged to come up with new restaurant concepts, and Moose Cafe is his latest venture. A refugee from the oil industry downturn in the '80s, Sadler originally opened The River Cafe, a casual bistro with al fresco dining in the Montrose area. After selling that, Sadler delved deeply into regional Mexican cuisine and opened Cafe Noche, which was built from the ground up on Montrose. With its pleasant patio, it is one of the most popular restaurants on Montrose "restaurant row."

Sadler's love of the Pacific Northwest, where he and his family go kayaking in British Columbia and hiking in the Cascade Mountains of Washington State, was the inspiration for Moose Cafe, which opened in December, 1995. The lodgelike restaurant features a sur-prisingly compatible marriage of subtle Pacific Northwest smoking and robust Texas barbecue. Dry herb and spice mixtures are used as rubs instead of oil marinades, and meats are slow-smoked at low tem-peratures for a healthier product.

Sadler and chef Alan Mallett, who learned the intricacies of Mexican cooking for Cafe Noche, have crafted a menu of refined home-style grills, sandwiches, salads, vegetables and desserts for Moose Cafe. State-of-the-art thermostati-cally controlled smokers slow-smoke everything from fresh shrimp and peppers skewered on rosemary branches to salmon, quail, beef and portobello mushrooms.

The sourdough bread baked daily is the descendant of a starter that has been passed down in the Sadler family for more than 130 years. His mother still makes bread every day, Sadler said.

Natural woods and earth colors, beamed ceilings, white maple tables and chairs create the feel of a Pacific Northwest lodge. The moose theme is reinforced subtly by a set of antique moose antlers over the bar, a decadent hazelnut coffee mousse garnished with moose antlers carved from chocolate, and Moosehead beer.

On pleasant days, a spacious patio with umbrella tables is a comfortable place to sit and watch the world go by.

LITE FARE

The slow cooking techniques used by Moose Cafe bring health benefits and delicious food. Meats are rubbed with herbs and spices rather than the traditional marinades that add fat. Vegetarian dishes include a Portobello Mushroom Burger, a Green Chile Sandwich and a Vegetable Plate. Ask that high-fat condiments be removed.

Moose Cafe
1340 W. Gray
Houston, Tx 77019
520-9696

SMOKED TOMATO AND SPINACH DIP

2	tablespoons clarified butter
1/2	cup chopped yellow onion
2	cups whipping cream
1	cup smoked tomatoes, peeled, seeded, cubed (see Special Helps section)
2	(8-ounce) packages cream cheese, softened (can use light)
1	cup creamy ricotta cheese
1/2	cup each: mayonnaise (can use light) and freshly grated Parmesan cheese
1	teaspoon each: chopped garlic, salt and white pepper
4	cups cooked chopped spinach or 2 (10-ounce) packages frozen, thawed

Heat butter in a 2-quart saucepan; sauté onion until translucent. Add cream; cook over medium heat until reduced by one-half. Remove from heat. Add tomatoes, cream cheese, ricotta, mayonnaise, Parmesan, garlic, salt, pepper and spinach; stir to combine.

Serving Suggestion: May be serve chilled or warm. To warm, microwave an 8-ounce ramekin 45 to 60 seconds on medium-high (70 percent). Serve with fried tortilla chips or toast points.

Makes 2 quarts, 16 (1/2-cup) servings.

Substitute evaporated skim milk for cream. Use fat-free: cream cheese, ricotta cheese and mayonnaise. Eliminate salt. Serve with baked tortilla chips, pita bread, low-fat crackers or fat-free bagel chips.

Gruet Brut (New Mexico) or Aria Brut (Spain); Roederer Estate Brut; J Sparkling Wine.

SPINACH QUESADILLAS

2 1/2	(10-ounce) packages frozen chopped spinach, thawed and well drained
2	cups shredded Monterey Jack cheese
1	tablespoon chopped garlic
1/2	teaspoon each: salt and freshly ground black pepper
24	(6-inch) flour tortillas
6	tablespoons oil

Combine spinach, cheese, garlic, salt and pepper in a medium bowl; blend well. Place a heaping tablespoon of mixture on half of a tortilla and fold over; fold again into quarters. Repeat with remaining spinach mixture and tortillas. Heat oil in a nonstick skillet; in batches, sauté quesadillas until lightly browned. Serve with sour cream and pico de gallo.

Serves 12 (2 each).

Cut out salt. Eliminate oil by sauteing quesadillas in a nonstick skillet using nonstick spray.

Vina del Mar Fume-Blanc (Chile); Torres Vina Sol (Spain); King Estate Pinot Gris (Oregon); Pinot Gris Domaine Zind Humbrecht Vielles Vignes (France).

SALMON CAKES

2 medium-size Russet potatoes, peeled
4 ounces raw salmon fillet, skinned and pin bones removed
2 ounces smoked salmon
1/4 cup finely chopped onion
2 tablespoons chopped garlic
1 teaspoon freshly ground black pepper
1/2 teaspoon salt
1/4 cup (1/2 stick) clarified butter (see Special Helps section)

Place potatoes, one at a time, through grating disk of food processor. Put potatoes in cold water; set aside. Add raw and smoked salmon, onion, garlic, pepper and salt to food processor bowl; pulse to blend until somewhat smooth. Transfer mixture to medium bowl. Drain potatoes well; pat dry. Pour off water but not starch which has settled to bottom. Add starch to potatoes; blend into salmon mixture.

Form into 8 (1/2-inch thick by 2 1/2-inch diameter) patties. Heat butter in a medium nonstick skillet; sauté patties 3 to 4 minutes on each side, over medium heat.

Serving Suggestion: Serve with salsa, beurre blanc or horseradish.

Serves 4.

 Eliminate salt and butter. Sauté salmon cakes in a nonstick skillet using nonstick spray.

White: Picpoul de Pinet (France); Freestone Sauvignon-Blanc; Domaine Ott Rose' (France).

Red: Chateau de Campuget Robert Kacher (France); Moulin des Sablons Chinon (France); Crichton Hall Pinot Noir.

LEMON CHESS PIE

1/2   cup (1 stick) butter
2   cups sugar
1   tablespoon each: all-purpose flour and cornmeal
1/2   teaspoon salt
2   tablespoons water
5   eggs
1/3   cup fresh lemon juice
   Zest of 2 lemons
1   (9-inch) unbaked pie shell
   Powdered sugar and strips of lemon zest dredged in sugar for garnish (optional)

Preheat oven to 350 degrees. Cream butter and sugar in electric mixer bowl. Add flour, cornmeal, salt and water; blend thoroughly. Add eggs, one at a time, beating until smooth. Stir in lemon juice and zest. Pour into pie shell. Bake 45 minutes, or until set. Cool at room temperature 30 minutes, then refrigerate covered. To serve, cut in wedges and sprinkle with powdered sugar. Garnish with strips of lemon zest.

Serves 8.

Relish a small bite.

Domaine Coyeaux Muscat de Beaumes-de-Venise (France); Taylor No. 10 Tawny Port (Portugal); Roullet V.S.O.P. (France). OK, it's a cognac, but try it!!

FACING PAGE, FROM LEFT: Pat McCarley, Rancho Tejas; Edi Maldonado, Viva!; Alan Mallett, Moose Cafe.

FOLLOWING PAGE, FROM LEFT: Luigi Ferre, Damian's; Melissa Bailey and Ben Bailey, Redwood Grill; Polo Becerra, Post Oak Grill.

ANCHO CHILI SOUP
BALSAMIC ANGEL HAIR PASTA WITH CHICKEN
NANTUCKET BLEU SPINACH SALAD
AMARETTO CHEESECAKE *with Amaretto Glaze and Chocolate Sauce*

Post Oak Grill is like a theatrical production — the lighting, decor and furnishings set the mood, and the food takes center stage. Owners Manfred Jachmich, a veteran Houston restaurateur with solid European training, and Ethel Fisher, a fourth generation Texan and third generation Houstonian with a grass roots regard for memorable comfort foods, are like producers who constantly revise and polish a hit show.

They recently added a Wine Room and Board Room to accommodate business and special-occasion gatherings. In the dining room, Toulouse Lautrec-style murals, garlands of lights entwined in real grapevines across the ceiling and cozy banquettes create a charming setting. The glass-enclosed atrium

is perfect for parties, and a piano bar offers dancing six nights a week. To many customers, Post Oak Grill is a home away from home for entertaining friends and business associates. Many have Post Oak Grill cater meals and parties. Week nights it is a neighborhood gathering place, but on weekends it draws an eclectic crowd from all over the city. Many loyal customers are acknowledged with brass name plates ringing the wainscoting.

Chef Polo Becerra has worked his way up in the kitchen and excels at American regional specialties sparked with Asian, Mediterranean, Latin and Southwestern touches. He delights in creating special-request dishes, and often they earn a place on the menu.

Redwood Grill, another Manfred Jachmich-Ethel Fisher enterprise, opened at its Montrose location in September, 1995 and already has become a destination restaurant for exciting dining. It is convenient for lunch after shopping or museum hopping in the area and for before- and after-theater dining. Earthy colors, a changing exibit of artwork and the Bombay Martini Room (a cozy bar with live piano music) create a welcoming atmosphere.

The American menu is executed with flair by executive chef Shelly Drought, a native Houstonian and graduate of the French Culinary Institute in New York, and pastry chef Melissa Bailey, graduate of the Culinary Institute of America.

Drought has worked at Gracie Mansion in New York, Honolulu, San Antonio, where she helped open Biga restaurant, and formerly was executive sous chef at Ruggles. Her fresh, seasonal menus blend Mediterranean, French, Asian and American regional flavors in fusion-style cooking. Specialties include grilled dishes, Nantucket Bleu Spinach Salad (spinach with bleu cheese, fresh blueberries, toasted pecans and blueberry vinaigrette); Texas quail stuffed with jalapeno cornbread with a smoked poblano sauce. Bailey already has earned acclaim for her sensational desserts.

Post Oak Grill
1415 S. Post Oak Lane
Houston, Tx 77056
993-9966

─────────── LITE FARE ───────────

Both Post Oak and Redwood Grill have a healthy food philosophy that extends to their menus. Sauces are made from reduced and pureed fresh fruits and vegetables rather than creams and other fats. Vegetarian items are available. Try the Vegetable Lasagna at Redwood Grill and the Black Bean Soup and Vegetarian Pasta at Post Oak Grill.

Redwood Grill
4611 Montrose Blvd.
Houston, Tx 77006
523-4611

POST OAK GRILL *and* REDWOOD GRILL

ANCHO CHILI SOUP

3 to 4   whole dry ancho chilies
1   small yellow onion, roasted (see notes)
1 to 2   garlic cloves
2   quarts chicken stock, divided
1/2   cup dry white wine
1   teaspoon each: fresh thyme and white pepper
1/2   cup instant potato flakes
1/4   cup light cream or 1 cup milk (see notes)
1/4   cup fat-free sour cream
   Salt to taste
1   cup crawfish or shrimp, boiled, peeled, deveined and chopped (optional)
   Sour cream for garnish

Roast chilies in a dry skillet over high heat until they become pliable and chile aroma is very pungent, 5 to 7 minutes. Stem and seed chilies; chop coarsely.

Finely chop roasted onion. Place garlic, onion and chilies in blender with a little stock; liquefy, adding as much stock as blender will hold. Pour contents of blender into remaining stock; reduce heat; whisk in wine, thyme, pepper and potato flakes. Simmer 10 minutes. Whisk in cream and sour cream. Add salt.

To give this soup a little something extra, add crawfish or shrimp 5 minutes before end of cooking.

To serve, place sour cream in a squeeze bottle and garnish each serving with a design of your choice.

Notes: Roast uncut onion in a 350-degree oven until brown, about 30 minutes. Less cream is needed because it is more concentrated.

Serves 6.

Good low-fat recipe. Use whole milk rather than cream and salt-free and defatted chicken stock.

Fall Creek or Llano Estacado Chenin-Blanc (Texas).

78

BALSAMIC ANGEL HAIR PASTA WITH CHICKEN

4	tablespoons olive oil
1 1/2	cups sliced mixed shiitake and white mushrooms
1/2	cup chopped fresh tomato
2	teaspoons minced garlic
1/2	cup each: balsamic vinegar and chicken stock
1	(2 1/2-pound) chicken, roasted, skinned, boned and cut into chunks
	Pinch of each: fresh oregano and red pepper flakes
	Salt and freshly ground black pepper to taste
1	pound dried angel hair pasta, cooked
1	cup freshly grated Parmesan cheese
	Chopped fresh parsley and Parmesan shavings for garnish

Heat oil in large skillet; sauté mushrooms, tomato and garlic. Deglaze pan (see Special Helps section) by stirring in vinegar and stock and scraping up any bits from the bottom. Add chicken, oregano, pepper flakes, salt and black pepper; toss with pasta and Parmesan. Garnish with parsley and shaved Parmesan.

Serves 4.

Limit oil to 1 tablespoon for sauteing. Use salt-free, defatted chicken stock. Substitute 4 (4-ounce) skinless, boneless chicken breast halves for whole chicken.

Barbera d'Asti Michele Chiarlo (Italy); Chianti Classico Nozzole or Brolio (Italy); Tignanello Antinori or Le Pergole Torte Monte Vertine (Italy).

NANTUCKET BLEU SPINACH SALAD

	Blueberry Vinaigrette (recipe follows)
2	bunches leaf spinach, stemmed, washed and dried well
1	pint fresh blueberries
2/3	cup crumbled Bleu cheese
1/2	cup chopped, toasted pecans

Prepare vinaigrette and set aside. In a large bowl, combine spinach, blueberries, cheese and pecans; toss with a generous amount of vinaigrette.

Blueberry Vinaigrette
Combine shallot, blueberries, sugar, salt, vinegar and oil in electric blender; puree until smooth. Toss with salad before serving.

Serves 6.

BLUEBERRY VINAIGRETTE

1	shallot, minced
1/2	pint fresh blueberries
3	tablespoons sugar
1	teaspoon salt
1/3	cup raspberry vinegar
1	cup vegetable oil

 Reduce cheese to 1/3 cup. Use only 1/2 cup oil in Blueberry Vinaigrette, using 2 tablespoons vinaigrette per serving.

 Enjoy without wine.

AMARETTO CHEESECAKE
with Amaretto Glaze and Chocolate Sauce

GRAHAM CRACKER CRUST

1 1/2	cups graham cracker crumbs
1/4	cup sugar
5	tablespoons melted butter

AMARETTO CHEESECAKE

3	(8-ounce) packages cream cheese, softened
3 1/2	cups firmly packed light brown sugar
1/4	cup granulated sugar
1/8	teaspoon salt
3	eggs
1/4	cup sour cream
1/2	teaspoon vanilla
1/3	cup amaretto liqueur
1/2	cup toasted, finely chopped almonds
	Amaretto Glaze (recipe follows)
	Chocolate Sauce (recipe follows)

AMARETTO GLAZE

1/4	cup (1/2 stick) butter
1/2	cup firmly packed brown sugar
1/8	teaspoon salt
1	cup amaretto liqueur, divided
2	cups powdered sugar, sifted
1	cup whipping cream

CHOCOLATE SAUCE

1	cup finely chopped semisweet chocolate
1	cup whipping cream

Graham Cracker Crust

Combine crumbs, sugar and butter until well blended. Grease a 9-inch springform pan; pack bottom with crumb mixture and set aside.

Amaretto Cheesecake

Preheat oven to 300 degrees. Beat cream cheese, sugars and salt until smooth and creamy in large mixing bowl. Add eggs, one at a time, beating well after each addition. Blend in sour cream, vanilla and amaretto; stir in almonds.

Pour into prepared pan. Set pan in water bath (a larger pan of hot water that comes to within 1/2-inch of top of baking pan). Bake 45 minutes, or until lightly golden and firm to the touch. Cool to room temperature; refrigerate covered several hours or overnight. To serve, release sides of springform pan and transfer cake to serving platter.

Amaretto Glaze

Combine butter, brown sugar, salt and 1/3 cup amaretto in medium saucepan over low heat. Cook just until the sugar melts and mixture is smooth. Remove from heat and cool about 5 minutes. Gradually add powdered sugar; beat until smooth. Beat in remaining 2/3 cup amaretto and cream to make a creamy glaze that can be drizzled over cake.

Chocolate Sauce

Place chocolate in small mixing bowl; set aside. Bring cream to a rapid boil in a small saucepan. Pour cream over chocolate; mix until melted and smooth.

Serves 12 to 16.

 Enjoy small portions of this treat and balance with a light entree.

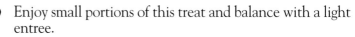 Fonseca Bin 27 Port (Portugal); Miles or Blandy's Malmsey Madeira (Portugal); Graham's, Taylor, Dow or Fonseca Vintage Port (Portugal).

STUFFED JALAPENOS CHIHUAHUAS
GRILLED STUFFED FLOUNDER
with Crabmeat Shrimp Stuffing and Tejas Pecan Butter
FRIJOLES A LAS CHARRAS POBLANOS
PECAN COBBLER

Rancho Tejas gives diners a taste of Texas history and Texas' best flavors in a contemporary ranch-house setting. Specialties of the Gulf Coast, South Texas, West Texas and Hill Country — Certified Angus beef, pecans, seafood, rice, 1015 onions, jalapenos and other chilies, fresh vegetables, pork, poultry and wines — turn up repeatedly in different, and delicious, guises.

Owner and native Texan, Pat McCarley, has improved on some of the legends. Chicken Fried Steak, for example, is made with round steak tenderized in a buttermilk marinade then breaded with a light sourdough "wash" and served with Cream Gravy; Pecan Pie is transformed into an outrageously rich cobbler topped with Blue Bell Homemade Vanilla ice cream.

"We are not trying to reinvent Texas food, but we are going to a lot of trouble to get quality products and give the food real Texas taste," he said.

McCarley's great-great-great grandfather, Samuel McCarley, set a precedent for the family's sense of Texas hospitality in 1836 by accommodating Gen. Sam Houston and 2,500 of his troops who stopped by his farm near the present-day Hempstead.

Today, Rancho Tejas is a stopping place for Houstonians entertaining friends and family and is a must for guests from out of town. You can dine in the central room or on the spacious front porch shaded by oak trees. Anyone who doesn't come hungry will quickly develop an appetite from the aromas of beef turning on the rotisserie and from breads, cookies and desserts baked in a glass-enclosed bakery in the entry.

McCarley, a graduate of the Conrad N. Hilton College of Hotel and Restaurant Management at the University of Houston, has worked in restaurants since he was 14; he is probably best-known as the director of operations for Goode Company restaurants for eight years.

Rancho Tejas has a sense of the wide open spaces. Architect Stephen A. Lucchesi researched West Texas forts built with native materials before designing this urban ranch house. It is distinguished by soaring, open-trussed ceilings of natural pine (the ceiling peaks at 26 feet), massive wood-burning stone fireplaces, murals and metal art. Lucchesi's wife, Amy, painted the ceiling-high sepia-toned mural wall depicting historic food scenes and regions of Texas, and McCarley's wife, Chris, worked on the interiors and designed the dried arrangements.

Opened in 1995, Rancho Tejas was named one of 14 best new restaurants in the nation by Bon Appetit magazine.

LITE FARE

Mesquite grilled lean meats and fish are tasty and healthy. Enjoy the 6-ounce beef tenderloin, chicken breast, red snapper or tuna steak. A Beef & Seafood Skewer combines chunks of mesquite grilled beef, fish and vegetables, served over rice and frijoles (check out this low-fat recipe). Choose the low-fat Honey Mustard dressing.

Rancho Tejas
4747 San Felipe
Houston, Tx 77056
840-0440

STUFFED JALAPENOS CHIHUAHUAS

1	(8-ounce) package cream cheese, softened
1/4	cup each, shredded: sharp Cheddar, Monterey Jack and Baby Chihuahua cheese
1/4	cup each, finely chopped: red bell pepper, roasted yellow onion (see note) and poblano pepper
2	tablespoons chopped cilantro leaves
2 1/2	teaspoons minced garlic
2	teaspoons seasoned salt
1/2	teaspoon each: garlic powder and freshly ground black pepper
3/4	pound shrimp, cooked, peeled, deveined and diced
24	mild pickled whole jalapenos Vegetable oil for deep frying All-purpose flour Jalapeno Batter Mix (recipe follows)

JALAPENO BATTER MIX

1	cup yellow cornmeal
1/2	cup all-purpose flour
1	teaspoon seasoned salt
2	eggs
1	cup water

Combine cream cheese, Cheddar, Monterey Jack and Baby Chihuahua cheeses thoroughly in large bowl. Add bell pepper, onion, poblano pepper, cilantro, garlic, salt, garlic powder, pepper and shrimp; blend well with a spatula.

Make a slit down one side of each jalapeno (wear plastic gloves if hands are sensitive) and scrape out seeds with a small spoon. Fill each jalapeno with stuffing (over-fill so that a 1/4-inch strip of filling shows in the slit). Refrigerate peppers until firm, at least 1 hour.

When ready to cook, pour at least 2 1/2 inches of oil into a heavy pot or deep fryer; heat to 350 degrees. Dust each jalapeno lightly with flour, then holding each pepper by the stem, dip into Batter Mix until fully coated. Drop immediately into hot oil and fry until golden brown. Remove from oil and drain on paper towels.

Serving Suggestion: Serve with salsa, ranch dip, guacamole and sour cream.

Jalapeno Batter Mix
Combine cornmeal, flour and salt in small bowl; mix thoroughly. In medium bowl, whisk eggs until frothy. Add water slowly to eggs; whisk well. Add cornmeal mixture to eggs; blend thoroughly. If not used immediately, chill well and stir again to blend before using.

Note: To roast onion: Peel and halve onion, place on a baking sheet, drizzle with olive oil and sprinkle with salt and pepper. Roast in 400-degree oven until browned, about 10 to 15 minutes.

Serves 8 (3 each).

 Substitute fat-free cream cheese for regular and use low-fat varieties of Cheddar and Monterey Jack cheeses. Eliminate salt.

Cold Mexican beer.

GRILLED STUFFED FLOUNDER
with Crabmeat Shrimp Stuffing and Tejas Pecan Butter

    Crabmeat Shrimp Stuffing
    (recipe follows)
    Tejas Pecan Butter (recipe
    follows)
  6 (8-to 10-ounce) fresh flounder
    fillets or other fresh fish
3/4 cup (1 1/2 sticks) melted
    butter, divided

CRABMEAT SHRIMP STUFFING
1/2 cup (1 stick) butter
1/2 cup each, finely chopped: onion
    and green bell pepper
1/4 cup finely chopped celery
1/2 pound shrimp, peeled, deveined
    and cut in half
  1 teaspoon chopped fresh thyme
1/2 teaspoon each: Creole mustard
    and salt
1/4 teaspoon each: paprika, red and
    freshly ground black pepper
  1 bay leaf
1/2 cup shrimp stock (see Special
    Helps section)
1/4 cup whipping cream
1/2 pound fresh crabmeat, cleaned
    and picked over
  2 cups cornbread, crumbled

TEJAS PECAN BUTTER
  1 cup shrimp stock (see Special
    Helps section)
  1 cup finely chopped onion
3/4 teaspoon minced garlic
1 1/2 cups (3 sticks) unsalted butter,
    divided
  2 tablespoons all-purpose flour
1/4 cup Worcestershire sauce
  2 teaspoons brown sugar
  1 teaspoon each: salt and bottled
    red pepper sauce
  2 cups toasted chopped pecans

Prepare Crabmeat Shrimp Stuffing; set aside. Prepare Tejas Pecan Butter; set aside.

Season fillets to taste; grill each using 2 tablespoons butter or oily based dressing to prevent fish from sticking to grill. Place warm Crabmeat Shrimp Stuffing on each plate, top with fillet and ladle hot Tejas Pecan Butter over fish and stuffing; serve immediately.

Crabmeat Shrimp Stuffing
Melt butter in a 2 1/2-quart saucepan; add onion, bell pepper and celery and sauté until soft. Add shrimp, thyme, mustard, salt, paprika, red and black peppers and bay leaf; cook 2 minutes over medium heat. Add stock; bring to a boil. Whisk in cream, add crabmeat and cook 2 minutes. Add cornbread; cook 2 minutes. Remove bay leaf. May be held covered in oven on warm setting until ready to use.

Tejas Pecan Butter
Combine stock, onion and garlic in 1-quart saucepan; bring to a boil; reduce heat and simmer 2 minutes. Set aside. Melt 4 table-spoons butter over medium heat in another 1-quart saucepan; whisk in flour. Whisking constantly, blend stock into butter mix-ture. Reduce heat to low and blend in remaining 1 1/4 cups butter, whisking constantly. Whisk in Worcestershire, sugar, salt and pepper sauce. Stirring frequently, add pecans and cook 5 minutes. Set aside.

Serves 6.

Serve 6-ounce fillets. Eliminate salt. Use salt-free, defatted shrimp stock. Limit butter to 1/4 cup for sauteing vegetables in Crabmeat Shrimp Stuffing and reduce cornbread to 1 cup in stuffing. In Tejas Pecan Butter, reduce butter to 1/2 cup, pecans to 1 cup and serving size to 1/4 cup each.

Kendall-Jackson Chardonnay Vintners Reserve; Fall Creek, Pheasant Ridge or Messina Hof Chardonnay Private Reserve (Texas); Meursault Genevrieres Remoissenet (France).

FRIJOLES A LAS CHARRAS POBLANOS

2	cups dry pinto beans
2 1/2	quarts chicken stock
1/4	pound smoked bacon, chopped
2	cups chopped yellow onions
1	cup chopped poblanos
1/2	cup chopped tomatoes
2	tablespoons cilantro leaves
2	teaspoons salt
1	teaspoon each: pinto bean seasoning mix or your favorite salt-free seasoning blend and freshly ground black pepper

Wash beans and soak in water 1 hour; drain. Place beans and stock in a 6-quart stockpot; bring to a boil. Reduce heat and simmer beans 45 minutes. Sauté bacon in a medium skillet until half done. Add onion, poblanos, tomatoes, cilantro, salt, seasoning mix and pepper; sauté mixture until vegetables are soft. Transfer vegetable mixture to stockpot with beans; simmer over low heat 45 minutes.

Note: Do not boil beans for an extended period of time or they will become cloudy.

Serves 8 to 10.

Use salt-free, defatted chicken stock. Eliminate salt.

Cold Mexican beer.

PECAN COBBLER

DOUGH

1 1/2	cups all-purpose flour
1	tablespoon dark brown sugar
1 1/2	teaspoons baking powder
1/2	teaspoon salt
1/4	cup (1/2 stick) plus 1 tablespoon cold butter, cut in pieces
1/2	cup whipping cream

FILLING

4	large eggs
1	tablespoon whipping cream
3/4	cup dark brown sugar
1/2	teaspoon salt
1/2	cup (1 stick) plus 1 tablespoon butter, melted
1 1/2	cups dark corn syrup
2	cups pecan halves

Dough
Combine flour, sugar, baking powder and salt in electric mixer bowl. Blend on low setting 3 minutes. Add butter, piece by piece, until a dry dough forms. Add cream; blend 3 minutes. Roll dough into a 1/8-inch thick rectangle to cover inside of a shallow 2-quart casserole. Press dough into casserole and trim edges.

Filling
Preheat oven to 350 degrees. Place eggs, cream and sugar in electric mixer bowl. Blend on low setting 3 minutes. Add salt, butter and corn syrup; blend 3 minutes. Stir in pecans. Pour filling into dough-lined casserole. Bake until lightly firm, about 45 minutes, turning pan midway through baking to ensure even cooking. Cobbler should be shaking when done; it sets somewhat as it cools.

Serving Suggestion: Serve warm in a bowl and top with a scoop of ice cream (the restaurant uses Blue Bell Homemade Vanilla). At the restaurant, the ice cream also is topped with a small shortbread cookie made from the same dough as the crust. The cobbler is like a syrupy pecan pie; the pecans float to the top as it bakes.

Serves 8 to 10.

Use moderation and balance this dessert with a low-fat entree.

Sounds scrumptious, but ice cream is so sweet and rich that it puts almost all dessert wines out of business. You could try pouring some Pedro Ximenez Sherry over the top before eating!

GRILLED SHRIMP *with Roasted Red Pepper Risotto*
PEPPER CRUSTED SEA BASS
with Kalamata Olives, Garlic, Capers and Tomato Ragout
GRILLED CENTER CUT PORK CHOPS *with Scotch Bonnet Fruit Chutney*
CAPONATA
WARM BITTERSWEET CHOCOLATE TORTE

A newcomer on the Houston dining scene, Riviera Grill quickly established itself as a fine-dining destination for contemporary Mediterranean cuisine that focuses on the French and Italian Rivieras. The restaurant has attracted a devoted following among Houstonians who normally would not venture outside the Loop — certainly not repeatedly. They are lured by scintillating dishes such as prawns wrapped in a crisp shell of kataifi, finely shredded filo dough that looks like shredded wheat; grilled sushi-quality yellowfin tuna and Chilean sea bass; polentas and risottos prepared to order; and luscious desserts such as a minitrio of creme brulees.

Owner/chef John Sheely is a native Houstonian and self-taught chef who believes in hands-on cooking. He dry-ages the Angus beef, dries the tomatoes, cures the salmon, makes his own stocks, sauces, desserts and breads (including an outstanding focaccia). Menus change seasonally to take advantage of the freshest and best produce, herbs and seafood.

Riviera Grill

Sheely graduated from Westchester High School and as a self-described "ski bum" moved to Colorado. He landed in Vail, where he worked in restaurants to support himself. Because he was too young to work upfront in restaurants that served alcohol, he ended up in the kitchens of several of Vail's best dining establishment. Sheely was a quick study and developed a fascination for innovative cooking.

He stayed in the ski resort 18 years, during which he married (he and his wife, Alicia, have two daughters) and owned the restaurant L'Ostello for two years. In 1994, the Sheelys decided they wanted to return to Houston, and they found a small space in a strip shopping center next to a movie theater. This rather unimpressive setting became the home for Sheely's impressive talent in August, 1995.

"If you really love what you are doing, it gets your creative juices flowing," said Sheely. He likes to work with ingredients that "just scream southern France" — garlic, tomatoes, roasted red peppers, artichoke hearts, capers and caper flowers, balsamic vinegar, eggplant and fresh herbs, especially thyme and basil.

Signature dishes include a Crispy Potato and Goat Cheese Tart with field greens (thinly sliced potatoes formed into a tart shell, filled with goat cheese, peppers and pine nuts, baked and then quickly sauteed); Portobello Mushroom Cake With Prosciutto; and Grilled Chicken With Sweet Roasted Garlic, Mashies (mashed potatoes) and Spinach.

LITE FARE

Riviera Grill's menu gives as much prominence to fresh vegetables, fruits and grains as it does to proteins. The flavors in fresh herbs, vegetables and fruits compliment the meats and starches. Try the recipe for Scotch Bonnet Fruit Chutney with pork. Risotto and pasta dishes are delicious. Enjoy great freshly prepared foods with little butter and cream.

Riviera Grill
9741 Westheimer
Houston, Tx 77042
974-4445

GRILLED SHRIMP *with Roasted Red Pepper Risotto*

3   tablespoons olive oil
1/3   cup minced onion
1 1/2   cups Arborio rice (Italian rice for risotto)
5   cups hot chicken stock, divided
1   teaspoon salt
    Freshly ground black pepper to taste
1   cup freshly grated Parmesan cheese, plus more for garnish
1/2   cup (1 stick) cold unsalted butter
1   cup roasted red peppers, julienned, plus more for garnish (see Special Helps section)
10   large shrimp (16/20 count), peeled and deveined
1/4   cup basil oil (see note)
    Kosher salt to taste

Note: For basil oil, process 1 cup packed fresh basil leaves in food processor until finely chopped, then blend in 1/2 cup extra-virgin olive oil.

Heat oil in saucepan; add onion and sweat (let cook until softened but not brown) 2 minutes. Add rice; stir 1 to 2 minutes, until well coated. Add 1/2 cup stock and cook, stirring constantly, until rice has absorbed most of the liquid. Simmer, adding remaining stock 1/2 cup at a time. Add salt and 1 teaspoon black pepper; continue to stir until liquid is absorbed and rice is tender but still slightly firm. Add Parmesan, butter and julienned pepper; stir until well mixed.

While risotto is simmering, marinate shrimp in basil oil, kosher salt and black pepper 5 minutes. Grill shrimp 3 minutes on each side. Risotto is done when most of the liquid has reduced and rice is creamy yet slightly firm. Sprinkle with Parmesan. Arrange shrimp over top of risotto in circular pattern. Garnish with red pepper strips.

Serves 2.

Sweat onion in a small amount of chicken stock. Use salt-free, defatted chicken stock. Reduce Parmesan to 1/2 cup. Cut butter to 2 tablespoons in risotto.

Viognier Duboeuf (France); Arrowood Saralee's Vineyard or La Jota Viognier; Chante Aloutte Chapoutier (France).

PEPPER-CRUSTED SEA BASS
with Kalamata Olives, Garlic, Capers and Tomato Ragout

2   (6-ounce) Chilean sea bass fillets
1/2   cup flour, mixed with 1 teaspoon each: paprika and freshly ground black pepper; and 1/2 teaspoon each: kosher salt and cayenne pepper
2   tablespoons plus 1 teaspoon olive oil, divided
6   Roma tomatoes, peeled, seeded and coarsely chopped
1   teaspoon chopped fresh basil
1   teaspoon each: minced garlic, sliced shallots and capers
8   kalamata olives
2   teaspoons julienned roasted red peppers
2   teaspoons fresh lemon juice

Preheat oven to 400 degrees. Dust fillets with flour mixture. Heat 2 tablespoons oil in ovenproof skillet and add fillets; sauté until both sides are browned. Place skillet in oven and roast 10 minutes. Remove from oven and cover with foil while preparing ragout.

Place remaining 1 teaspoon oil in another ovenproof skillet and add tomatoes, basil and garlic; toss to coat. Place skillet in oven and roast 15 minutes. Remove from oven and let cool slightly.

Return to stove top and add shallots, capers, olives and red peppers; bring to a simmer. Serve the fish over ragout and top with fresh-squeezed lemon juice.

Serves 2.

Use just 1 tablespoon oil for sauteing. Cut olives to 4.

Lachryma Christi Mastroberardino (Italy); Domaine Ste. Michelle Brut (Washington); Iron Horse Brut Rosé Sparkling Wine; Chateau de Beaucastel Blanc (France).

GRILLED CENTER CUT PORK CHOPS
with Scotch Bonnet Fruit Chutney

Zest of 1 each: large lime and lemon (see Special Helps section)
Zest of 2 medium navel oranges (see Special Helps section)

1	cup boiling water
1/2	tablespoon sugar
2	medium kiwi
1	medium mango
1	small pineapple
1/4	cup white wine vinegar
1/4	cup sugar
1/2	cup finely diced yellow onion
1	large red scotch bonnet pepper (habanero)
	Kosher salt and freshly ground black pepper to taste
6	(10-ounce) center-cut pork chops
	Salt and pepper to taste
	Extra-virgin olive oil

Blanch lime, lemon and orange zest in boiling water with 1/2 tablespoon sugar 1 minute over high heat. Strain and reserve.

Peel, seed and dice all citrus, kiwi, mango and pineapple. Combine with zest and reserve. Combine vinegar and remaining 1/4 cup sugar in 2-quart stainless steel saucepan. Stirring frequently, cook over medium-high heat until sugar caramelizes and turns a light mahogany color, about 10 minutes.

Carefully, to avoid splattering hot sugar mixture; add onion and scotch bonnet pepper. Cook 1 minute over low heat. Add fruit and zest mixture. Stirring occasionally, simmer 10 minutes over low heat. Sugar will harden but simmering and stirring will melt it again.

Carefully strain mixture through sieve. Reserve juice (about 1 1/2 cups). Return juice to same saucepan and reduce by one-half over medium heat. When reduced, pour over fruit mixture and mix well. Season with salt and pepper. Set aside at room temperature. Serve warm or cold with any grilled items (hot with pork, cold with fish).

Season pork with salt and pepper on both sides. Brush with extra-virgin olive oil. Grill over charcoal briquets heated to gray ash. Place on rack over coals; cook 10 minutes per side to medium done. Or, broil in oven 15 minutes per side, turning only once.

To serve, put each chop on a plate. Spread chutney over half of chop. Serve with risotto (mix some of the chutney with risotto on plate) and garnish with fried sweet potato chips.

Serves 6 to 8.

 Great recipe but decrease pork portion to 6-ounce chops and don't rub with oil.

White: Fall Creek Emerald Riesling (Texas); Niersteiner Riesling Spatlese (Germany); any Vendange Tardive Gewurztraminer or Riesling (Alsace).

Red: Cotes-du-Rhone Guigal (France); Truchard Zinfandel; Ridge Lytton Springs Zinfandel.

CAPONATA

This is a slightly different version of caponata that is wonderful served as a vegetable with the sea bass, or as an appetizer. Excellent sprinkled with balsamic vinegar and crumbles of chevre (goat cheese).

1/2	cup finely diced yellow onion
4	garlic cloves, cut into thirds
6	tablespoons extra-virgin olive oil, divided
1	large eggplant (unpeeled), diced into 1/2-inch cubes
2	teaspoons each: kosher salt and finely ground black pepper

Preheat oven to 400 degrees. Combine onion, garlic and 4 tablespoons oil in ovenproof skillet and sweat (let cook until softened but not brown) 15 minutes over medium heat. Add eggplant, salt, pepper and remaining 2 tablespoons oil; sauté over medium heat 15 minutes. Place skillet in oven and roast 20 minutes. Remove from oven and stir 3 or 4 times. Return to oven 10 to 15 minutes before serving.
Serves 2.

 Use just 1 tablespoon oil and 1/2 teaspoon salt.
Enjoy with same wines as bass.

WARM BITTERSWEET CHOCOLATE TORTE

7	ounces each: bittersweet chocolate and unsalted butter (2 sticks less 2 tablespoons)
1 3/4	cups powdered sugar
1	cup all-purpose flour
3	eggs plus 4 egg yolks Fresh berries for garnish

Preheat oven to 450 degrees. Combine chocolate and butter in top of double boiler and melt over simmering water (do not let water touch bottom of pan). Sift sugar and flour into a medium mixing bowl.

In a separate large bowl, whisk eggs and egg yolks together. Whisk warm chocolate mixture into eggs. Fold flour mixture into egg-chocolate mixture with a spatula.

Spoon mixture into 6 (4-inch) buttered, floured aluminum tart pans or spray with nonstick vegetable spray. (Can be refrigerated as long as 4 hours if you would like to make ahead.) Bake 7 to 9 minutes if mixture is at room temperature, or 10 to 12 minutes if mixture is cold, until centers are still quite soft. Invert each tart onto a plate. Serve with ice cream, vanilla sauce (creme anglaise) and raspberry sauce (pureed, sweetened raspberries). Garnish with fresh berries, if desired.

Serves 6.

 Enjoy this recipe in moderation.

Asti Spumanti Cinzano (Italy); Blandy's or Miles Malmsey Madeira (Portugal); Brown Brothers Reserve Muscat (Australia).

ACORN SQUASH SOUP
STUFFED DOVER SOLE
TOURNEDOS VORONOFF
BLANC MANGE ROMANOFF

The Rivoli provides the ultimate Continental dining experience — classic food prepared with flair, fine wines, polished service and an elegant setting. For more than 20 years Houstonians, their guests and international visitors have been dining and entertaining at the Rivoli for everything from birthday luncheons to business dinners. Private rooms can accommodate parties of various sizes from intimate dinners in the Wine Cellar to events for 80 in the Wine Room, Piano Room or Garden Room. Glennie Scott, a Houston favorite, performs nightly in the Piano Room.

Continuity is the Rivoli's key to success — the current owners, sisters Rosalinda Soto and Rosi Cantu, have been there since the restaurant opened in 1975: Soto was a pantry girl and Cantu, an accounting assistant. They bought the restaurant in 1994. Pierre Gutknecht, a European-trained chef, also has been there from the start, and eight of the 12 kitchen staffers have been employed for 12 years or more.

Gutknecht is from Neuchatel, Switzerland where his family owned a small hotel. He began his training at 18 and worked in fine Swiss hotels in Zurich and Lausanne; he is a graduate of the Ecole Hotelier School. After coming to the United States in 1970, he worked at several private clubs and restaurants. His forte is the classics — Escargot Bourguignonne, Tournedos, Rack of Lamb, Chateaubriand with bouquetiere of vegetables, Dover Sole, Calf Sweetbreads Princess (with lump crab, asparagus and beurre blanc), Calf's Liver Veronique (a top favorite at the Rivoli), French Onion Soup, Vichyssoise and Lobster Bisque.

Gutknecht has updated the menu with risottos, grilled swordfish, salmon, shrimp and softshell crab entrees and is pleased to honor special requests, especially for heart-healthy dishes. The emphasis is on freshness. Rosalinda Soto's mother, Emma Ocanas, grows herbs for the kitchen in a back garden. The Rivoli is especially memorable for its dessert souffles and desserts prepared at tableside such as Bananas Foster, Cherries Jubilee and Crepes Suzette as well as its excellent wine list.

The ambiance adds to any dining occasion; a cherub fountain at the entrance is filled with floating roses and rose petals, a romantic theme repeated throughout. Leaded glass doors open onto a setting highlighted by a wine rack cabinet filled with Baccarat crystal decanters and the Rivoli's collection of fine Cognacs; a handsome Oriental screen; lattice and paneled walls; lace curtains; paintings; and fresh flowers (arranged by Rosi Cantu).

Rivoli

───────── *LITE FARE* ─────────

Chef Pierre personalizes his food preparation to the tastes and dietary needs of his customers. Special requests are expected and honored. Fresh fish can be grilled, poached or steamed. Sauces can be served on the side. A steamed vegetable platter is an off-the-menu option. Just ask, and your special request will be filled.

Rivoli
5636 Richmond Ave.
Houston, Tx 77057
789-1900

ACORN SQUASH SOUP

8   (3 1/2-inch diameter) acorn
    squash with stems
2   (1 1/2-pound) acorn squash
2   medium onions, sliced
3   cups chicken stock
1   cup whipping cream
1/2 teaspoon ground nutmeg
    Salt and freshly ground black
    pepper to taste

Cut a slice from the bottom of each small squash so that they will sit level. Cut off tops; reserve for lids. Scoop out seeds and enough pulp so that each squash will hold 3/4 cup soup. Reserve pulp for soup.

Preheat oven to 350 degrees. Peel, seed and cut large squash into 2-inch chunks. Combine with reserved pulp, onion and stock in a 3-quart saucepan. Cook over medium heat 15 minutes or until squash is tender. Working in batches, place squash and stock in food processor; blend until smooth. Return squash puree to saucepan; add cream, nutmeg, salt and pepper. Heat to serving temperature.

Fill squash shells with water; place shells on a baking sheet; bake 15 minutes. Drain water; fill shells with soup. Garnish with nutmeg; cover with squash lids.

Serving Suggestion: Can be garnished with lump crabmeat or sauteed pecan pieces. May also be served chilled or for a thinner soup, add more stock.

Serves 8.

Use salt-free, defatted chicken stock. Substitute half-and-half for cream.

Carmenet Colombard-Blanc; Lustau Les Arcos Dry Amontillado-Sherry (Spain); Miles or Blandy's Sercial Madeira (Portugal).

STUFFED DOVER SOLE

4 (16- to 20-ounce) whole Dover sole, skinned and trimmed (about 9 ounces each)
Salt and freshly ground black pepper to taste
All-purpose flour, divided
2 tablespoons oil
1 tablespoon butter
3 small shallots, finely chopped
1 garlic clove, finely chopped
4 large white mushrooms
2 artichoke bottoms, sliced
3/4 pound lump crabmeat, picked over and cleaned
1 cup whipping cream
1/4 cup dry white wine
Fresh lemon juice to taste
1 bunch chives, chopped
Garnish: paprika, Brown Butter (see note), 4 lemon halves, watercress sprigs

Season sole with salt and pepper; dust with flour. Heat oil in medium skillet; sauté sole 2 to 3 minutes each side or until done; set aside and keep warm. Melt butter in same skillet; sauté shallots and garlic; add mushrooms, artichokes and crabmeat. Sprinkle lightly with flour. Blend in cream and wine; stir over medium heat until mixture thickens. Season with salt, pepper and lemon juice. Stir in chives.

With sharp knife, cut down the center of each sole to separate fillets; set aside. Lift bone out and dip or sprinkle with paprika. Fill cavity of sole with crabmeat stuffing, top each with 1 tablespoon Brown Butter and garnish with bone, lemon half and watercress.

Note: For Brown Butter, melt 4 tablespoons butter in hot skillet; add a dash of lemon juice and Worcestershire sauce; stir until brown. Do not let burn.

Serves 4.

Limit oil to 1 tablespoon for sauteing in a nonstick skillet and eliminate butter. Substitute half-and-half for cream. Eliminate Brown Butter.

Lalande Chardonnay Robert Kacher (France); Hautes Cotes de Beaune Jayer Gilles (France); Deloach Chardonnay O.F.S. or Chateau Montelena Chardonnay; Montrachet Marquis de la Guiche Joseph Drouhin (France).

TOURNEDOS VORONOFF

4   (6- to 8-ounce) beef tenderloin steaks
    Salt, freshly ground black pepper
    and cayenne pepper
2   tablespoons oil
1/4 cup each, chopped: shallots and
    fresh parsley
1   garlic clove, chopped
1   tablespoon all-purpose flour
1   tablespoon beef stock
1/4 cup each: Cognac or brandy and
    Madeira wine
1   tablespoon paprika
1/2 cup demi-glace or brown sauce
    (see Special Helps section)
1   cup whipping cream
    Juice of 1 lemon
2   teaspoons Dijon mustard

Season tournedos with salt, black and cayenne peppers. Heat oil in a medium skillet; sauté tournedos over medium heat about 2 minutes per side. Remove from skillet when rare or medium rare. Add shallots, parsley, garlic, flour and stock to skillet; sauté, then return tournedos to skillet and flame with Cognac. Remove tournedos to a warm platter. Deglaze skillet with Madeira; add paprika, demi-glace and cream. Reduce over medium heat to a sauce consistency; whisk in lemon juice and mustard. Pour sauce over tournedos.

Serving Suggestion: Accompany with green beans, carrots, broccoli, grilled red bell pepper, asparagus spears, rice and French bread. Serves 4.

Limit beef portion to 6 ounces. Eliminate oil by sauteing tournedos in a nonstick skillet using nonstick spray. Substitute evaporated skim milk for cream.

Napa Ridge or Dunnewood Cabernet Sauvignon; Torres Gran Coronas Reserva Black Label (Spain); Chateau Bourgneuf (France) or Truchard Merlot; Chateau Latour or Mouton-Rothschild (France).

BLANC MANGE ROMANOFF

1   quart milk
1   cup sugar
3   envelopes unflavored gelatin
     dissolved in 1/3 cup cold water
2   tablespoons amaretto liqueur
1   tablespoon almond extract
2   teaspoons vanilla
     Pinch of salt
2   cups whipping cream, whipped
     Romanoff Sauce (recipe
     follows)
     Toasted sliced almonds
     Whipped cream and fresh mint
     leaves and berries for garnish

ROMANOFF SAUCE

1 1/2 pints fresh strawberries or
      raspberries
3/4   cup sugar
1/4   cup strawberry or raspberry
      liqueur
      Juice of 1/2 lemon

Bring milk and sugar to a boil in a 1 1/2-quart saucepan. Remove from heat and whisk in dissolved gelatin, amaretto, almond extract, vanilla and salt. Cool over pan of ice. When mixture becomes the consistency of mayonnaise, fold in whipped cream. Pour into 10 to 12 (6-ounce) molds or custard cups. Chill until set, about 1 to 2 hours. Dip mold in hot water briefly to loosen and unmold. Pour Romanoff Sauce on plate; top with blanc mange and almonds. Garnish with whipped cream, mint leaf and fresh berries.

Romanoff Sauce

Combine berries and sugar in a 1 1/2-quart saucepan; bring to a boil. Remove from heat and cool. Add liqueur and lemon juice; puree in blender.

Serves 10 to 12.

 Savor a small portion.

Moscato d'Asti Stefano (Italy); Newlan Riesling Late Harvest; Arrowood Riesling Late Harvest; Far Niente Dolce.

MEDALLIONS OF VENISON *with Chile-Pepper Sauce*
SMOKED CHICKEN SALAD *with Papaya Salsa*
PRALINE ICE CREAM PARFAIT *with Caramelized Pecans and Chocolate Sauce*

No list of the best restaurants in Houston would be complete without the Rotisserie for Beef and Bird, which has consistently been recognized for outstanding food, wines and service since it opened in 1978.

Owner/chef Joe Mannke, who trained in fine hotels and restaurants in Europe and South Africa, has extended his knowledge and expertise to American regional cooking. He was executive chef at Anthony's Pier 4 in Boston (the largest-volume restaurant in the U.S. at the time). He also was the chef in charge of Disney World's seven kitchens when it opened (supervising more than 125,000 meals daily) before coming to Houston as chef of the Hyatt Regency Hotel.

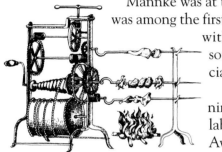

Mannke was at the forefront of the American regional cooking trend in this area and was among the first local restaurateurs to feature game specialties such as wild boar along with roast goose, duck, pheasant and quail. He uses local and area sources whenever possible for the freshest products, but brings in specialties from all over the country.

The restaurant has received the Wine Spectator Grand Award for nine consecutive years; the Wine Cellar boasts 18,000 bottles from 850 labels. The restaurant also has received the DiRona Award and the Ivy Award of Distinction from Restaurants and Institutions Magazine and has been named to Restaurants and Institutions Magazine's Hall of Fame for Fine Dining. It is repeatedly ranked among the Zagat Survey's top five restaurants in Houston for food, wine and service.

Rotisserie for Beef and Bird

Holidays are especially festive at the Rotisserie. The Colonial architecture and oil paintings, used brick walls, handcrafted oak tables, rotisserie and hearth and cozy Hunt Room with a fireplace are a natural background for the traditional American Thanksgiving feast for which the staff dresses in Indian or Colonial costumes. It has become so popular that there is almost always a waiting list even though Mannke has increased the seatings.

Valentine's, Mother's Day, Easter and Secretaries' Day are other sell-out events. The restaurant also hosts wine-tasting events and has three rooms to accommodate private parties.

LITE FARE

Rotisserie for Beef and Bird specializes in healthy, fresh and delicious foods reaped from Texas' farms and wildlife. Wild game, game birds and fresh seafood are typically lean and can be grilled dry or with just a touch of olive oil. Steamed vegetables and wild rice, high in fiber and B vitamins, make great accompaniments to the grilled meats.

Rotisserie for Beef and Bird
2200 Wilcrest
Houston, Tx. 77042
977-9524

SMOKED CHICKEN SALAD *with Papaya Salsa*

1	head Boston bibb lettuce
2	heads Romaine
3	whole chicken breasts, smoked or grilled
2	cups Papaya Salsa (recipe follows)
4	hard-cooked eggs, cut into quarters
1/2	cup pitted black olives
4	Roma tomatoes, quartered
2	dozen fresh, long chives or parsley sprigs
1	cup Italian dressing

Wash greens in lots of cold water; shake and dry thoroughly, then chill. Line a salad bowl or platter with chilled bibb lettuce. Cut Romaine across into 2-inch chunks; place in bottom of bowl or platter. Cut chicken off the bone, remove skin and cut chicken into strips; arrange over lettuce. Spoon Papaya Salsa around edge of dish and garnish with eggs, olives, tomatoes and chives. Just before serving, pour Italian dressing evenly over salad.

PAPAYA SALSA

2	ripe papayas
1	each, small: red and green bell peppers
1	serrano pepper; seeded and chopped
1	cup Fruit Sauce (recipe follows)

Papaya Salsa

Peel papayas, discard seeds and dice into small cubes. Cut peppers into halves, discard seeds and chop finely. Combine papayas, bell peppers, serrano and Fruit Sauce in chilled bowl. Use as directed.

FRUIT SAUCE

1/2	cup orange marmalade
1/4	cup each: fresh lemon and orange juices
2	tablespoons prepared horseradish
1/2	teaspoon each: ground ginger and dry mustard powder
1/4	teaspoon salt, or to taste

Fruit Sauce

Combine marmalade, lemon and orange juices, horseradish, ginger, mustard and salt in blender; puree until smooth. Use as directed.

Note: This delicious sauce also may be served with cold seafood, game or pates.

Serves 4 to 6.

🍎 Reduce eggs to 2 and substitute a fat-free Italian dressing for regular.

🍇 Beringer White Zinfandel; Callaway Viognier; Veuve Clicquot Demi-Sec Champagne (France).

MEDALLIONS OF VENISON *with Chile-Pepper Sauce*

12	(2-ounce) venison medallions, from the back-strap if possible
4	egg whites, whipped
2	tablespoons soy sauce
1	teaspoon honey
2	garlic cloves, minced
2	tablespoons cornstarch
1/2	cup each: vegetable oil and soft butter (1 stick)
	Chile-Pepper Sauce (recipe follows)

Pound venison medallions with a mallet; place in a ceramic dish. Combine egg whites, soy sauce, honey, garlic and cornstarch in a small bowl. Spoon mixture over venison, combine well and refrigerate 24 hours.

Remove medallions from marinade. Heat oil in a medium skillet; sauté medallions over high heat on both sides until nicely brown. Do not overcook; meat should be pink in the center. Add butter to give venison a delicious nutty taste. Remove venison from skillet, place on a heated platter and set aside. Keep skillet with butter and venison pan drippings on stove to make Chile-Pepper Sauce.

Serving Suggestion: Ladle Chile-Pepper Sauce over venison; serve with wild rice or risotto and winter vegetables.

CHILE-PEPPER SAUCE

3	strips bacon, sliced
1/2	each, medium-size, diced: yellow onion, red and green bell peppers and jalapeno, seeded and minced
2	cups sliced portobello mushrooms
2	tablespoons chili powder
1	teaspoon all-purpose flour
1/2	teaspoon ground cumin
2	cups beef stock or consomme
1/2	cup dark red wine (cabernet sauvignon)
1/4	cup dry sherry
1	cup whipping cream
	Salt, freshly ground black pepper and cayenne pepper to taste

Chile-Pepper Sauce

Sauté bacon in venison pan drippings. Add onion, bell peppers, jalapeno and mushrooms; sauté until glossy. Sprinkle with chili powder, flour and cumin; combine well. Add stock, wine and sherry; bring to a boil. Reduce heat and simmer for a few minutes, then add cream. Heat, but do not boil.

Serves 4.

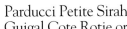 Use low-sodium soy sauce. Eliminate oil by sauteing venison in a nonstick skillet using nonstick spray. Reduce butter to 1/4 cup. Use salt-free, defatted beef stock and substitute half-and-half for cream in the Chile-Pepper Sauce.

Parducci Petite Sirah; Gigondas Paul Jaboulet (France); Guigal Cote Rotie or Hermitage (France).

PRALINE ICE CREAM PARFAIT
with Caramelized Pecans and Chocolate Sauce

6 egg yolks
1 quart whipping cream (chill cream, bowl and beaters well)
1/4 cup sugar
1/2 cup each: honey and bourbon
Caramelized Pecans (recipe follows)
Chocolate Sauce (recipe follows)
Fresh strawberries and mint leaves for garnish

Place egg yolks in large bowl; set aside. Whip cream until stiff; set aside. Combine sugar and honey in a small saucepan; bring to a boil, reduce heat and simmer about 2 minutes. Remove from heat and whisk slowly, a little at a time, into egg yolks. Continue whisking until yolks are cool; add bourbon and mix well. Fold in whipped cream; combine with Caramelized Pecans.

Line a 10x4x4-inch bread pan or terrine with plastic wrap; pour in parfait mixture. Freeze overnight. Dip pan in hot water; unmold parfait onto a chilled platter. Slice into serving portions, pour a generous amount of Chocolate Sauce onto each dessert plate and place a slice of the parfait in center of sauce. Garnish with strawberries and mint.

CARAMELIZED PECANS
1 1/2 cups sugar
1/4 cup water
1 cup pecan pieces

Caramelized Pecans

Combine sugar and water in a heavy 2-quart saucepan; bring to a boil over high heat. Continue boiling until sugar turns a light brown. Add pecans; combine well. Remove from heat; carefully pour onto a cookie sheet lightly coated with nonstick spray. Allow to cool, then "chop" pecans with a rolling pin.

CHOCOLATE SAUCE
1 cup whipping cream
1/2 cup each: sugar and chopped bittersweet chocolate (such as Belgian)
1/2 cup Kahlua (coffee liqueur)
6 tablespoons butter

Chocolate Sauce

Combine cream, sugar, chocolate, Kahlua and butter in a heavy 1 1/2-quart saucepan; bring to a boil. Reduce heat and simmer 10 minutes, or until sauce starts to thicken. Set aside. Cool to room temperature before serving.

Serves 6.

Enjoy in moderation.

Serve with coffee.

FACING PAGE, FROM LEFT: Rosalinda Soto and Pierre Gutknecht, Rivoli; Hessni Malla, La Tour d'Argent; Greg Torres, Cavatore.

FOLLOWING PAGE, FROM LEFT: Mark Cox, Tony's; Jeff Vallone, Grotto; Jon Paul, Tony's; Bruce McMillian, Anthony's.

ROASTED PEPPERS WITH FONTINA
OSSO BUCO *with Balsamic Vinegar and Risotto alla Milanese*
PENNE PASTA WITH ARUGULA
CHICKEN POSITANO *with Italian Spinach*

Tony Vallone, Houston's most high-profile restaurateur, offers a range of dining experiences in his award-winning restaurants — from Tony's, the city's top culinary and social see-and-be-seen venue, to sophisticated Anthony's; two Grottos, which feature southern Italian cooking; and La Griglia, an Italian grill. All feature wood-burning ovens. After a 15-month closure and renovation, Tony's reopened for dinner only in 1995. The redesign coordinated by Michael J. Siller Interiors encompasses a resplendent red and coral interior, undulating wall of exotic wood, handpainted frescoes and paintings with accents of ebony, brass, lacquer, travertine and granite. Table appointments include stunning Versace china plates and Riedel Austrian crystal.

The revamped menu of eclectic continental food with strong Italian overtones was created by Vallone and executive chef Mark Cox after visiting three-star restaurants in Europe and New York. Hallmarks are opulent presentations and only-the-best fresh produce and locally grown herbs, seafood, hand-cut meats,

fish, free-range chicken, hearth-roasted game and a world-class collection of wines. Nightly specials focus on in-season rareties such as squash blossoms, white truffles and exotic mushrooms. Guests know to save room for Tony's signature desserts such as white chocolate and raspberry vacherins, Elizabeth's Praline Cheesecake and souffles. Food also is available at the full-service bar, where a grand piano provides background for lively happy hours.

The two Grotto restaurants are run by Vallone's son, Jeff, and specialize in more casual Neapolitan food with "a lot of soul," according to chef Marco Wiles. Vallone's son, Joey, who ran La Griglia, has moved to Dallas and opened his own restaurant, Joey's. A children's menu is a recent addition at Grotto. Pasta, pizza and broiled chicken are popular lunch and dinner specials. Pastas for all Vallone restaurants are hand-made in the pasta room.

The high-energy atmosphere begins in the entry with its prominent bar backed by a wood-burning pizza oven and is enhanced by mural walls by Jan Parsons. The Focolari Ladi (Fireplace Room) seems cozy by contrast. Grotto is usually filled with loyal customers who return often for Margherita pizza, Calamari Toto (named for an uncle), Oysters Mimmo, Panzarotti sandwiches and Aranchini rice balls, to name a few popular specials. The dessert cart features a tempting array of chocolate desserts such as Brownie Toffee Cake and Mezzanotte (Midnight) Cake along with Elizabeth's Cheesecake, Strawberry Cassata and the signature Key Lime Pie.

Tony's
1801 Post Oak Blvd.
Houston, Tx 77056
622-6778

Grotto
3920 Westheimer
Houston, Tx 77027
622-3663

──────────── LITE FARE ────────────

While the Mediterranean menu at the Grotto offers foods acclaimed as the healthiest diet in the world, Tony's upscale menu presents a light philosophy of food preparation. Healthy choices include Veal-Stuffed Pasta in Vegetable Broth, Sea Bass in Cartoccio and for dessert, Torta di Fragole and Homemade Assorted Italian Ices.

Grotto
6401 Woodway
Houston, Tx 77057
782-3663

ROASTED PEPPERS WITH FONTINA

2   large red bell peppers
1/2 pound fontina cheese, shredded
1/2 serrano pepper, finely minced
2   tablespoons chopped fresh basil
1/2 teaspoon each: freshly cracked
     black pepper and cayenne
     pepper
15   (1-inch) pieces anchovy fillets
     Flour for dredging
2   eggs, whipped slightly
     Olive oil

Char bell peppers over a charcoal grill or under the broiler until skin begins to blister. Place in plastic or paper bag 10 to 15 minutes to sweat. Remove skin and seeds; cut into 1x3-inch strips. Combine cheese, serrano pepper, basil, black and cayenne peppers in a bowl; blend thoroughly. Top each pepper strip with 1 tablespoon of cheese mixture and 1 piece of anchovy; roll into a cylinder. Dredge prepared peppers in flour, then dip into whipped egg mixture. Heat oil in medium skillet; sauté peppers until golden brown. Serve immediately.

Serves 6 to 8.

🍎 Enjoy in moderation.

🍇 Enjoy without wine.

OSSO BUCO
with Balsamic Vinegar and Risotto Alla Milanese

4   thick (3 1/2-inch diameter)
      veal shanks (about 22 ounces
      each), trimmed of fat —
      see note
      Salt and freshly ground black
      pepper to taste
      All-purpose flour
8   tablespoons extra-virgin Italian
      olive oil, divided
1 1/2 cups finely chopped carrots
6 to 8 garlic cloves, minced
1   (28-ounce) can imported
      Italian tomatoes (with liquid)
4   tablespoons tomato paste
1   red onion, finely chopped
2   cups chicken stock
1 1/2 cups dry white wine
1 1/2 cups sliced exotic mushrooms
      (oyster, shittake, portobello,
      porcini)
1/2   cup balsamic vinegar
6   tablespoons chopped fresh
      parsley

Season veal shanks with salt and pepper; dredge in flour. Heat 6 tablespoons oil in a roasting pan or casserole large enough to hold shanks in one layer. Brown shanks well on both sides, about 5 minutes over medium-high heat. Arrange shanks, bone up, in the pan. Add carrots, garlic, tomatoes and liquid, tomato paste and onion. Pour in stock and wine; stir well. Cover pan, reduce heat and let simmer gently about 2 1/2 to 3 hours.

Heat remaining 2 tablespoons oil in a small skillet; add mushrooms and sauté 2 to 3 minutes. Add to shanks along with vinegar. Correct seasoning if needed; stir well and simmer 5 minutes. Sprinkle with parsley; serve immediately.

Note: Meat may have to be special ordered from your butcher.

Serves 4.

🍎 Reduce oil to 1 tablespoon to sauté veal shanks in a nonstick skillet using nonstick spray. Use salt-free, defatted chicken stock. Plenty of meat for 8 servings.

🍇 Barbera d'Alba Michele Chiarlo (Italy); Barbaresco Marchesi di Gresy or Ceretto (Italy); Barolo Pio Cesare or Bruno Giacosa (Italy).

RISOTTO ALLA MILANESE

3	tablespoons olive oil
1	cup minced onion
2	teaspoons minced shallots
2	cups Arborio rice
2	cups dry white wine (such as chardonnay)
1	tablespoon ground saffron
5	cups hot chicken or beef stock
1 1/2	teaspoons salt
2	tablespoons butter, cut into bits
1/2	cup freshly grated Parmigiano Reggiano cheese
	Freshly ground pepper

Heat oil in heavy, nonreactive skillet such as stainless steel. Saute onion and shallots until golden. Add rice and stir to coat with oil. Add wine; stir well and let simmer, stirring occasionally, until wine is absorbed. Add saffron, then 1/2 cup stock and salt. Cook, stirring constantly, until all stock has been absorbed.

Continue adding hot stock in small amounts (just enough to completely moisten rice) and cook, stirring constantly, until all has been absorbed and rice mixture is creamy and thick. Remove risotto from heat. Whip in butter and half the grated Parmesan. Season with salt and pepper. Top each serving with more grated Parmesan to taste. Serve immediately with Osso Buco.

Serves 6.

 Great low-fat recipe. Use salt-free, defatted chicken stock.

PENNE PASTA WITH ARUGULA

1/4	cup extra-virgin olive oil
1	pound assorted fresh mushrooms (shiitake, crimini, portobello, porcini, etc.), sliced
2	tablespoons minced garlic
4	heaping cups chopped fresh Roma tomatoes, about 6 to 8 large
1	teaspoon sugar
1	pound dry penne, fusilli or ziti pasta, cooked al dente
1/2	cup freshly grated Parmesan cheese
4	bunches arugula (leaves only, cleaned)
1/2	cup fresh sweet basil, torn in pieces
1/2	cup toasted pine nuts
	Crushed red pepper flakes
	Additional Parmesan for the table

Heat oil in a large skillet over medium heat. Add mushrooms and garlic; while stirring, sauté about 2 minutes. Add tomatoes and sugar; stir and lightly sauté about 3 minutes. Cook pasta; drain. In a large warm bowl, toss pasta, tomato sauce, 1/2 cup Parmesan, arugula, basil and pine nuts. Mix well; add a generous pinch of red pepper flakes; toss again. Serve at once with extra pepper flakes and Parmesan at the table.

Serves 4.

 Limit oil to 1 tablespoon to sauté vegetables.

Chianti Rufina Frescobaldi (Italy); Rosso di Montalcino Avignonesi (Italy); Chianti Classico Riserva Isole e Olena (Italy); Chianti Classico Riserva Badia Passignano Antinori (Italy).

CHICKEN POSITANO *with Italian Spinach*

6 (6-to 8-ounce) boneless, skinless chicken breast halves
3 cups shredded mozzarella
1/2 cup freshly grated Romano cheese
1 cup ground hot Italian sausage, cooked, drained and cooled
1/2 cup diced red bell pepper, cooked and cooled
1/2 cup hand-torn fresh basil leaves (each leaf torn into 4 or 5 pieces)
2 cups all-purpose flour
6 eggs, lightly beaten
3 cups Italian-seasoned bread crumbs
2 tablespoons olive oil
   Marsala Wine Sauce (recipe follows)
   Italian Spinach (recipe follows)

MARSALA WINE SAUCE
2 teaspoons olive oil
1 red onion, chopped
3 cups dry marsala
2 cups veal stock (or beef stock — see Special Helps section)
   Salt and freshly ground black pepper to taste
2 tablespoons butter

ITALIAN SPINACH
5 pounds fresh leaf spinach, washed, stemmed and dried
1/2 cup extra-virgin olive oil
2 teaspoons chopped garlic
   Salt and freshly ground black pepper to taste

Preheat oven to 350 degrees. Lay chicken breast flat on cutting board, skin side down, and pound slightly until thickness of breast is equal. Repeat with remainder of breasts. Combine mozzarella, Romano, sausage, peppers and basil in a medium bowl; mix thoroughly. Place about 1/2 cup of cheese mixture on half of each breast. Roll the other half of breast over the cheese mixture and squeeze to completely seal all edges. Dredge each stuffed breast in flour; dip in egg and coat with bread crumbs.

Heat oil in a medium skillet; sauté all sides of stuffed breasts until golden brown. Bake 8 to 10 minutes, or until cheese begins to ooze from sealed edges. Cut each breast into slices and fan over a pool of Marsala Wine Sauce.

Marsala Wine Sauce
Heat oil in a 2-quart saucepan; sauté onion until soft. Add wine and simmer until reduced to half, about 10 to 15 minutes. Add stock, let reduce to half again, about 15 to 20 minutes. Add salt and pepper; whisk in butter, and strain.

Italian Spinach
Sauté spinach in hot oil, add garlic and stir until wilted. Add salt and pepper.

Serving Suggestion: Arrange chicken and spinach on plate; top with strips of roasted red and yellow bell peppers.

Serves 6.

Prepare 4-ounce chicken breast halves. Cut mozzarella to 1 1/2 cups and eggs to 3. Use just 2 tablespoons oil in Italian Spinach.

White: Soave Pieropan or Cantina Sociale di Soave (Italy); Wolf Blass or Penfold's Chardonnay (Australia); Far Niente Chardonnay.

Red: Beaujolais-Villages Jadot or Duboeuf (France); Cotes-du-Rhone-Villages Guigal (France); Joseph Phelps Vin du Mistral Le Mistral; Chateauneuf-du-Pape Chateau Rayas or Chateau de Beaucastel (France).

VIVA!

VIVA! BLACK BEANS, BLACK BEAN BURRITO
RANCHERO SAUCE
VIVA! PASTA
SPINACH ENCHILADAS
PEACH MELBA SMOOTHIE

Viva! offers Mexican food without the guilt — all your favorite specialties — enchiladas, tacos, tamales, burritos and beans — with the flavor but without the grease and fat. Opened in 1995 by Roger Liebrum, a residential and commercial land developer turned restaurateur, Viva! combines the best of traditional Mexican fare with a consciousness of today's concerns about health and fitness.

Canola oil replaces lard; low-fat sour cream, cheeses and yogurt are used instead of the regular high-fat, high-cholesterol products; brown rice is steamed in vegetable stock to enhance the flavor, and entrees are made with boneless, skinless chicken breasts, marinated lean beef, fish and seafood. Even tamales are made without lard. However, the chili con queso and guacamole are made the traditional way and so is a deliciously wicked flan. The menu also features vegetarian versions of most entrees as well as herbal teas, specialty coffees and several low-fat desserts.

Flavor comes from cooking techniques and the use of fresh herbs, seasonings, fresh vegetables, chilies and low-fat condiments, said chef Edi Maldonado. He started at the former Tila's and also has worked for Cafe Express and Seekers health food stores.

Viva! offers the festive and relaxed ambience of a Mexican hacienda with Saltillo tiles, antique brick walls and khaki and rust accents. A rotating exhibit of paintings, photographs and sculpture from Circa Now Gallery and other artists provide a constantly changing background, and you can buy the art right off the walls.

The Spanish-style courtyard with its pleasant fountain, plants and lush landscaping is a great place to enjoy a sunny or cool day or evening and gather with friends on weekends.

The restaurant is a favorite with families as well as neighborhood regulars and Mexican food fans who come from the Rice Village, Medical Center and all over the central and southwest area. Sunday breakfast is a big attraction.

Signature dishes include Ranchero Sauce (ask for it warm with chips as an alternative to salsa), fresh salsa, Peach Melba Smoothie, Black Bean Burritos, Stone-Ground Blue Corn Tortilla Nachos, Vegetarian Nachos and Tamales, Viva! Pasta with black beans, Spinach Low-Fat Pepper Jack Quesadillas and Breakfast Fajitas (grilled turkey sausage, roasted peppers and onions on a sizzling platter with migas, rosemary potatoes and flour tortillas), Huevos Quesadillas and pancakes (plain, banana pecan and raspberry).

──────── LITE FARE ────────

This delightful restaurant is making a concerted effort to bring credibility to traditionally high-fat Mexican food. By substituting low-fat foods for regular and optimizing the intrinsic flavor of the traditional foods, fat and sodium are reduced. Look for designated low-fat and vegetarian items. Try the healthy and delicious recipes included here.

Viva!
2491 S. Braeswood
Houston, Tx 77030
666-2491

VIVA! BLACK BEANS

2   (15-ounce) cans black beans
1/2 cup water
1   tablespoon vegetable bouillon
      granules
1   cup diced white or yellow onion
2   tablespoons minced garlic
1   tablespoon ground cumin
1/2 tablespoon sea salt
2   tablespoons olive oil

Place beans with their liquid in a large saucepan. Add water, bouillon granules, onion, garlic, cumin, salt and oil; bring to a boil. Simmer over low heat about 30 minutes; watch carefully so beans do not scorch. Use in Viva! Pasta and Black Bean Burrito or as a vegetable.

Serves 4.

 Pretty low-fat as is, but can be prepared without oil.

BLACK BEAN BURRITO

1   (12-inch) low-fat whole-wheat
      flour tortilla or other burrito
      tortilla
1/2 cup each: Viva! Black Beans
      (recipe precedes) and Ranchero
      Sauce (recipe follows)

Heat tortilla on both sides in large, hot skillet until soft. Do not use oil. Place tortilla flat on counter and place beans in center. Fold tortilla over beans and roll loosely. Some beans may come out the ends, but that's OK. Place burrito on plate and pour Ranchero Sauce over top.

Serves 1.

 Use fat-free tortillas.

 Faustino $\underline{V}$ Reserva (Spain); Marques de Riscal Rioja (Spain); Marques de Murrieta Reserva Rioja (Spain).

Ranchero Sauce

4	very ripe large (8- to 12-ounce) tomatoes
1/4	cup olive oil
1/2	teaspoon salt
1	tablespoon minced garlic
1/4	cup each: sliced bell pepper and yellow or white onion
1	(14 1/2- or 15-ounce) can peeled whole tomatoes
1	bay leaf
1/2	teaspoon crushed oregano
1/4	teaspoon ground cumin

Place tomatoes in roasting pan and roast at 450 degrees until tops are burned dark, about 30 to 45 minutes (bottoms will remain moist). Let cool. In blender or food processor, lightly puree roasted tomatoes and juices from pan.

Combine oil, salt, garlic, bell pepper and onion in a 2-quart saucepan; saute over medium heat until onion is clear. Add roasted tomato puree and canned tomatoes. Simmer over low heat about 10 minutes. Add bay leaf, oregano and cumin; simmer over low heat 20 minutes; remove bay leaf.

Note: This versatile sauce can be served with tortillas and chips or on burritos, enchiladas, tamales or quesadillas. At Viva! it is served warm with chips as an alternative to salsa.

Makes generous 1 quart, 8 (1/2-cup) servings.

 Reduce oil to 1 tablespoon.

Viva! Pasta

2	tablespoons olive oil
	Pinch of salt
1	teaspoon minced garlic
1	tablespoon chopped cilantro
1	large tomato, diced
2	tablespoons white wine
1	cup Viva! Black Beans (recipe precedes)
8	ounces cooked pasta
2	tablespoons freshly grated Parmesan cheese

Heat oil in a small skillet over medium, heat. Add salt, garlic, cilantro and tomato; cook 1 to 2 minutes. Add wine and beans; saute to reduce liquid to desired consistency. Pour mixture over cooked pasta and garnish with Parmesan.

Variation: If desired, add grilled shrimp or chicken (1/2 to 1 boneless, skinless chicken breast per serving.)

Serves 1.

 Reduce oil to 1 teaspoon for sauteing.

 Quinta de Parrotes Periquita (Portugal); Beyerskloof Pinotage (South Africa); Pesquera (Spain).

SPINACH ENCHILADAS

1   (10-ounce) bag fresh spinach
1   teaspoon olive oil, divided
1   teaspoon minced garlic
1/4 small yellow onion, diced
1/4 teaspoon salt
1/8 teaspoon freshly ground black pepper
6   ounces low-fat pepper jack cheese, shredded
6   (6-inch) corn tortillas
    Salsa of choice

Wash spinach well and remove stems. Heat 1/2 teaspoon oil in a medium nonstick skillet. Saute garlic and onion over medium heat until onion is transparent. Add spinach, salt and pepper; cook only until spinach is wilted and mixed well with other ingredients. Remove from heat and drain well. Set aside.

To roll enchiladas easily, add remaining 1/2 teaspoon oil to skillet and lightly fry tortillas (see note) until they are warm and soft. Divide spinach mixture among tortillas. Divide cheese among tortillas. Roll tortillas and top each with favorite salsa.

Note: To warm tortillas in microwave, wrap 6 tortillas in damp paper towels. Microwave on high 45 seconds.

Serves 3 (2 enchiladas each).

Enjoy this low-fat and healthy recipe.

Chateau Ste. Michelle Semillon (Washington); Chateau Moncontour Vouvray (France); Sparr or Trimbach Pinot Gris (France).

PEACH MELBA SMOOTHIE

6   ounces frozen peaches (without added sugar), thawed
1   tablespoon raw honey
1/2 banana (2 ounces), cut into chunks
1/2 cup ice

Combine peaches, honey, banana and ice in blender; puree to desired texture.

Serves 1.

Healthy and refreshing. Enjoy!

LINDA MCDONALD, M.S., R.D., L.D.

Linda McDonald, food and nutrition consultant, is dedicated to helping people eat healthy in all situations. Her nutrition tips, recipe modifications, and nutritional analysis of recipes in "Houston Is Cooking The Best" will demonstrate that food can be tasty and healthy.

Linda holds a Master's Degree from the University of Texas Graduate School of Biomedical Sciences and a Bachelor's Degree from the University of Houston. She is active in The American Dietetic Association, president of the Houston Area Dietetic Association, past-chairman of the Consulting Nutritionists, and past director of the Texas Dietetic Association Foundation. Linda was honored by the American Heart Association for development of the first Houston Area Dining Out Guide, Heart Healthy Houston, in 1988 and is serving on the Board of Directors of the American Heart Association, Houston Division.

As a consultant to the restaurant and food industry, as well as corporate wellness programs, Linda's unique expertise has enhanced menus, food products, and educational materials. She is a popular speaker on nutrition topics for consumers and professionals. This is the eighth book that has been enhanced with her nutrition expertise.

HEALTHY RECIPE MODIFICATIONS *by Linda McDonald, M.S., R.D., L.D.*

The secret to healthy eating is to enjoy foods that not only taste good but are good for you. No food or recipe is "good" or "bad". How an individual food or recipe fits into a total diet determines the health benefits. Understanding food and learning how to use basic principles of balance and moderation is smart eating.

The LiteFare tips, recipe modifications and nutrition information are provided to help you make informed choices. Use the nutrient analysis chart to check the difference between the original recipe and the modified version. Then decide whether to use the suggested modifications based on your particular health needs and your eating plans for the rest of the day. Remember that balance and moderation are the keys to eating healthy.

RECIPE MODIFICATIONS

Recipes are usually modified to change one or more of the ingredients so that the outcome is more beneficial. The four basic reasons for modifying recipes are:

- To reduce fat and cholesterol.
- To reduce sodium.
- To reduce sugar.
- To add fiber.

A recipe can be modified in four ways:

- Eliminate an ingredient.
- Change the amount of an ingredient.
- Substitute one ingredient for another.
- Change the cooking method.

TO REDUCE FAT & CHOLESTEROL:

Limit the portion of meat, fish or poultry to 3-4 ounces per serving. The current dietary recommendations are to eat no more than 6 ounces of lean meat, poultry or fish per day.

Choose lean cuts of meat and trim all visible fat before cooking. This includes removing the skin of poultry, which can be done before or after cooking. If you are using a moist cooking method (stewing, boiling, covered casserole), remove the skim before cooking. If using a dry cooking method (baking, broiling, grilling), leave the skin on during cooking to keep the product from drying out, but remove the skin before eating.

Plan a variety of proteins - animal and vegetable. Cycle red meat, poultry, and fish with dried beans, peas and lentils.

Marinating lean cuts of meat tenderizes them by breaking down muscle fiber. This is done by the acid part of the marinade - vinegar, wine, pineapple juice, etc. Oil is not necessary. Prick the meat all over with a fork to allow the marinade to penetrate thoroughly.

Use non-fat or 1 percent dairy products. Replace whole milk cheese with cheese made from skim milk, such as part-skim milk mozzarella. Try some of the new low-fat cheeses.

Prepared meats and cheeses should have no more than 5 grams of fat per ounce. Check the labels or ask the grocer where you shop.

Use sharp cheddar and other strong tasting cheese. Place cheese on top to have the strongest influence on your taste buds.

Low-fat cooking methods include broiling, baking, roasting, poaching, and stir-frying. Utensils for low-fat cooking are non-stick cookware, vegetable cooking spray, and steamers.

Saute with broth, wine or water instead of oils or butter.

Microwave vegetables in a covered dish with just a small amount of water, rather than sauteing in oil or butter.

Make stocks, soups, sauces, and stews ahead of time. Chill, then remove all hardened fat from the top. If there is no time to do this, skim off as much fat as possible. Then add several ice cubes. The fat will congeal and cling to the ice cubes, which can be discarded.

If you can't make your own stocks, look for low-fat and low-sodium canned beef or chicken broth. Be sure to defat canned broth by chilling until fat hardens, then skim off.

Use fewer egg yolks and whole eggs in cooking. Substitute two egg whites for each whole egg.

Use eggless pasta in place of egg pastas. Most dry pastas are eggless, and most fresh pastas use eggs, but check the ingredient labels.

Use nuts, seeds, olives, cheese, butter, margarine, and oils in moderation.

Olive and canola oils are the best choices for cooking. Use olive oil for sauteing and salad dressings, choose canola for baking. But remember that these are still fats.

Try the following low fat substitutions:
Cream — 1/3 cup non-fat dry milk in 1 cup skim milk or canned evaporated skim milk.

Sour Cream — Non-fat yogurt or 1 cup no-fat or 1% cottage cheese + 1 tablespoon lemon juice, blended.

Mayonnaise — 1 cup plain non-fat yogurt and 1/2 cup Lite mayonnaise.

To Reduce Salt and Sodium:

Salt is an acquired taste. Your taste for salt will diminish as you gradually reduce the amount you use. You will begin to enjoy the taste of the food rather than the salt.

Add salt last, after tasting the food. Use just enough to correct food's flavor. Remove the salt shaker from the table.

Nothing else tastes exactly like salt, but other seasonings can enhance the flavor of foods and compensate for the salt you eliminated. Use the following seasonings to add zest to foods:

Lemon or Lime Juice — use on salads and cooked vegetables. For more juice, microwave for 30-60 seconds before juicing.

Citrus Zest — the thin outer layer of an orange, lemon or other citrus peel. Adds flavor to baked goods, sauces and other dishes. Use a zester or grater.

Flavored Vinegars — (tarragon, raspberry, wine)

Dried Onion Flakes, Onion or Garlic Powder, Garlic Cloves

Condiments — Worcestershire sauce, hot pepper sauce, mustard, soy, etc. are relatively high in sodium, but if used sparingly, can enliven foods without overdoing the sodium.

Herbs — Fresh herbs have the best flavor, but if not available, substitute 1/2 to 1 teaspoon dried herb per tablespoon of fresh herb. Crush the dried herb to release the flavor.

Wines & Liqueurs — If cooked at or above boiling temperature, the alcohol evaporates, eliminating most of the alcohol and calories while the flavor remains.

Salt can be eliminated or reduced in all recipes except yeast breads where salt is necessary to control the growth of the yeast. Even in yeast breads, salt can usually be reduced; one teaspoon per tablespoon of dry yeast.

Use salt-free or low-sodium canned products. Rinse canned products such as beans with water before using.

Salt is not necessary in the boiling water when cooking pastas, rice or other grains.

To Reduce Sugar:

Sugar can be reduced by one-third to one-half in most recipes. In cookies, bars and cakes, replace the sugar you have eliminated with non-fat dry milk.

Brown sugar or honey are sweeter than sugar, and may be substituted for white sugar using a considerably smaller amount. Nutritionally they are all the same, so there is no advantage to brown sugar or honey.

Flavor can be enhanced with spices (cinnamon, nutmeg or cloves) and extracts (vanilla, almond, orange or lemon). Doubling the amount of vanilla a recipe calls for will increase the sweetness without adding calories. Be careful about increasing spices to boost flavor when sugar is decreased. Cloves and ginger can easily overpower the recipe. Safest spices to increase are cinnamon, nutmeg and allspice.

When reducing sugar in a recipe, substitute fruit juice for the liquid or add fruits such as raisins, dried apricots, dates or bananas. Frozen orange or apple juice concentrate can be added. One tablespoon concentrate equals 1/4 cup fresh juice.

To Add Fiber:

Use more whole grains (bulghur, brown rice, corn, barley and oatmeal), vegetables, dried beans, split peas and lentils.

Substitute whole wheat flour for white flour whenever possible. It is heavier than white flour, so use less; 7/8 cup whole wheat flour for one cup white flour. Experiment to find out what works best in recipe. Some recipes will turn out well with all whole wheat flour, others are better when half whole wheat and half white flour is used.

Add wheat bran, oat bran, oatmeal or farina to baked products, cereals, casseroles, and soups. Start with one or two tablespoons and increase gradually. Substitute up to 1/2 cup oatmeal or oat bran for part of the flour in baked goods.

Use unpeeled potatoes whenever possible in soups, stews or for oven fries.

Use whole grain pastas and brown or wild rice.

SPECIAL HELPS

Some terms and recipes from restaurant owners and professional chefs may be unfamiliar to home cooks. Here are several terms that you may see frequently.

Achiote – a yellow seasoning and color from the seeds of the annatto tree. Used in Central and South American, Indian, Mexican and Southwestern cooking.

Ancho chilies – dried poblano peppers; dark reddish brown, about 4 inches long.

Brown Sauce (Sauce Espagnole) – one of the foundation or "mother" sauces of French cooking; the base for many other sauces. Here is an easy recipe.

    2   tablespoons oil
    1   small onion, finely chopped
    1/2 carrot, grated
    1   tablespoon finely chopped fresh parsley
         Pinch of dried thyme
    1   bay leaf
    1 1/2 tablespoons all-purpose flour
    1 1/2 cups beef stock or bouillon
         (see Beef Stock recipe that follows, use
         canned or dissolve 1 teaspoon instant bouil-
         lon granules in 1 1/2 cups boiling water.) Salt
         and freshly ground black pepper to taste

Heat oil in large skillet. Add onion, carrot, parsley, thyme and bay leaf. Stir in flour and simmer slowly until browned, about 10 minutes. Whisk in stock, season to taste (don't over-salt) and simmer about 2 minutes. Strain. Makes about 1 1/2 cups.

Capers – the small green berry-like buds of the caper bush used as a condiment or to give piquant flavor to sauces. Usually available bottled or pickled in vinegar.

Chipotle – Dried, dark red smoked jalapeños.

Chocolate – To melt in the microwave: place chocolate in a glass dish and melt on medium (50-percent) power, about 1 1/2 to 2 minutes per square, stirring midway through. Chocolate may not look melted; test by stirring to smooth.

Clarified butter – Often used in delicate, fine dishes because it doesn't burn as easily as whole butter. Melt butter (preferably unsalted) over low heat until foam disappears from top and sediment and milk solids collect in bottom of pan. Pour off clear butter; discard sediment.

Concasse – crushed, seeded fruit or vegetables, especially tomatoes.

Confit – (confee) – cooked meat (usually duck or goose) preserved under a layer of fat.

Coulis – (coulee) – pureed mixtures of fruits or vegetables.

Cream – when chefs list cream as an ingredient, they usually mean heavy cream of at least 36 percent butterfat.

Heavy cream is usually labeled whipping cream. When whipped, it doubles in volume. Most whipping cream now is ultra-pasteurized for longer shelf life. Better texture and optimum volume are achieved if the cream, bowl and beaters are thoroughly chilled before the cream is beaten. Some supermarkets stock heavy whipping cream.

If light cream is specified, look for cream labeled coffee cream or table cream.

Deglaze – Pour off all but a tablespoon or two of accumulated fat from sauteed food; add stock, water, wine or liquid called for in the recipe and simmer, scraping up browned bits from bottom of pan with a wooden spoon.

Demi-glace (DIM-ee-glahs) – A rich, brown suace based on basic espagnole (see Brown Sauce listing above). It is mixed with beef stock and sherry or madeira and simmered slowly until reduced by half to a thick glaze. Often used as the base for other sauces and as a glaze added to the pan at the last minute.

End Hunger Network – Many of the hotels and restaurants in this book contribute unused or specially prepared food to the End Hunger Network, a world wide alliance of private and volunteer organizations committed to ending hunger in the world by the year 2000. The Houston Chapter sponsors the Red Barrel program of food collection in hundreds of local supermarkets and the End Hunger Loop, which collects food from restaurants and food service institutions and distributes it to area missions and shelters. Call 963-0099 for information.

Herbs – Fresh are preferred if of good quality. The rule of thumb in substituting dried herbs is one teaspoon dried for three teaspoons fresh.

Nopales – fleshy pads of the cactus (nopal) that also produces prickly pears (cactus pears).

Olive oil – Extra-virgin olive oil is preferred by most chefs because it is the finest quality and has distinctive flavor. It is used for salad dressings or uncooked dishes and is not suitable for frying, as are lower grades of olive oil, because it has a low smoking point.

Less expensive grades such as superfine virgin, virgin or "pure" are better for everyday use. Store olive oil in a cool, dark place.

Pasta – Make your own or purchase from supermarkets or pasta shops. Fresh pasta is best with light, fresh tomato sauces or delicate cream sauces; dried pasta, with heartier, long-simmered meat and red sauces. Fresh pasta takes only 3 to 5 minutes to cook; dried may take as long as 15 minutes. Pasta should always be cooked "al dente," which means firm to the tooth. It should lose its floury taste, but not be hard or mushy. Rinse cooked pasta with tepid water if holding it to serve later. Rinse in cold water if using in salads.

Plunge strainer of pasta into hot water to revive it, then drain and serve. For best quality, hold pasta in cold water no longer than 30 minutes.

Roasted Garlic – Remove the papery outer skin, but leave heads of garlic whole. Slice off about 1/4-inch of top. Place in one layer in baking dish that has a cover; drizzle with olive oil or dot with butter. Cover pan and roast at 350 degrees until cloves are soft, about 45 minutes. Use in recipes or separate cloves and squeeze to extract garlic pulp. Discard skins. Spread garlic on bread rounds or toasted French bread or use in dressings. Four heads of garlic yield about 1/4 cup.

Alternatively, wrap each head of garlic in aluminum foil and bake at 350 degrees 1 hour. Let cool 10 minutes.

Roasted Peppers – To roast fresh peppers, rinse and dry, place on a baking sheet in a 350-degree oven 7 to 10 minutes (or broil 4 to 5 inches from heat 5 minutes on each side, until surface of peppers is blistered and somewhat blackened.) Drop into ice water and let sit for a few minutes until skins rub off easily. You can also place roasted peppers in a paper bag or plastic bag and let sit until skins rub off easily.

Handle jalapeños and other hot chilies with care as peppers and fumes can irritate skin and eyes. Wearing rubber gloves is recommended. Removing walls and seeds of peppers cuts the heat.

Roasted Tomatoes – Rub tomatoes with olive oil and place on a baking sheet. Put in oven and roast at lowest setting (warm) 8 to 10 hours. Remove tomatoes from oven, peel and seed.

Reduce – Cook a mixture down slowly until reduced by half or the amount specified. In contemporary cooking, reductions are frequently used to concentrate flavors or thicken sauces instead of thickening with flour or other starches.

Roux – A mixture of flour and fat that is the thickening base for many sauces and soups, particularly gumbo. The usual method is to heat oil until it is at the smoking point, then to whisk in flour and stir constantly until mixture is a dark mahogany brown, almost black.

Roux requires close attention; it must be stirred or whisked almost constantly for 45 minutes to an hour or it will burn.

It is much easier in the microwave. The following method is from newspaper microwave columnists Ann Steiner and CiCi Williamson in their first book, *"Microwave Know-How:"*

Heat 1/2 cup each oil and flour in a 4-cup glass measure. Microwave on high (100-percent) power 6 to 7 minutes, stirring every minute after 4 minutes, until a deep brown roux is formed.

Stock – Stocks made on the premises are the rule in professional kitchens. If you use canned broths, buy a good quality produce. Avoid salty broths, purchase low-sodium broth or reduce salt in the recipe.

When making stock at home, use a non-aluminum pan. For clear stock, skim foam and scum off top as it accumulates. Stir as little as possible to prevent clouding. Stock should simmer slowly, not boil. Cool quickly (setting the pan of stock in a container or sink of cold water speeds the cooling process). Chill, then remove congealed fat from top. Refrigerate or freeze.

Beef or veal stock: Combine 2 to 4 pounds beef bones and meaty soup bones or veal bones and trimmings (brown half the meat) in a saucepot. Add 3 quarts cold water, 8 peppercorns, 1 each: onion, carrot and celery rib, cut in pieces; 3 whole cloves, 1 bay leaf, 5 sprigs parsley and other desired herbs such as dried thyme.

Bring to a boil and skim off foam. Simmer covered 3 hours, skimming occasionally. Strain stock, cool quickly and refrigerate or freeze. When cold, remove

any solid fat that has risen to the top; remove fat before freezing.

Chicken stock: Place 3 pounds bony chicken parts in a stockpot with 3 quarts cold water, a quartered onion stuck with 2 whole cloves, 2 each: celery ribs and carrots; 10 peppercorns, 5 sprigs parsley and 1 bay leaf. Cover pot, bring to a boil over medium heat, then reduce heat and simmer stock partially covered, 2 to 3 hours.

For clear stock, skim off foam and scum on the surface. Add salt to taste after about 1 hour. Strain stock and discard bones and solids. Let cool. Refrigerate or freeze when cool.

Fish stock: Place 2 pounds fish bones, trimmings and head in a stock pot. Add 2 quarts cold water, 1 each: thinly sliced onion and peeled carrot; 10 white peppercorns, a large bay leaf, a sprig of thyme, 10 parsley sprigs and 1 teaspoon salt. Bring to a boil, reduce heat and simmer covered about 1 hours. Strain through a fine strainer, cool quickly and refrigerate or freeze. Makes about 1 3/4 quarts.

Shrimp stock: Place shells from 1/2 pound of shrimp in saucepan with water to cover. If desired add a little salt, parsley, crumbled dried thyme and a bay leaf (or make a bouquet garni of herbs tied in a cheesecloth bag). Bring to a boil, reduce heat and simmer 10 to 15 minutes. Strain and use or cool quickly and refrigerate or freeze.

Sweat – Place chopped vegetables or other ingredients in a partially covered pan over low heat and heat until moisture beads form and vegetables are softened.

Vinegar – Use clear white vinegar unless recipe specifies another type such as cider, fruit-flavored, rice wine or balsamic vinegar (dark, aged Italian vinegar).

Zest – The thinnest colored part of the peel only (no pith or white membrane); usually refers to citrus fruit.

SHOPPING GUIDE

Houston abounds in sources for ethnic and special ingredients called for in recipes in *"Houston Is Cooking The Best"*. Specialty supermarkets are stocked with exotic produce; fresh herbs; special sauces; condiments; spices; flavored oils and vinegars; juices; pastas; breads; pastries; frozen patty shells and filo dough; canned imported items as well as a wide variety of coffees and teas.

Ethnic markets run the gamut from Mexican to Middle Eastern, Caribbean, Chinese, Japanese, Korean, Vietnamese, Thai and Indian. Visiting these markets makes for interesting weekend excursions.

Bakeries such as **French Gourmet** (three locations) sells ready-made puff pastry dough in addition to specialty breads, cakes and other pastries.

Houston is fortunate to have a number of fine bread bakeries including **Big Sky Bread Company,** 5314 Weslayan; **Empire Baking Company** (two locations); **French Riviera Bakery & Cafe,** 3032 Chimney Rock; **Great Harvest Bread Company,** 5403 FM 1960 West; **la Madeleine** (several locations); **La Victoria,** 7138 Lawndale; **Le Moulin European Bakery,** 5645 Beechnut; **Le Notre** (three locations); **Manna Bread Company,** 2815 Dulles Ave. in Missouri City; **Moeller's Bakery,** 4201 Bellaire Blvd.; **Patisserie Descours,** 1330-D Wirt Road; **Stone Mill Bakers** (two locations); **Three Brothers Bakery** (three locations); and **Whole Foods Markets** (three locations).

GENERAL

Auchan, 8800 W. Sam Houston Parkway, Houston, 77099, 530-9855. A hypermarket stocked with a United Nations of imported foods from around the world including hundreds of cheeses; international wines; spices; fresh produce; meats; seafood and fish; a full range of grocery items; and baked goods from the in-store bakery.

Fiesta Marts, more than 40 locations. Excellent source for fresh produce and foodstuffs from the world's markets — baked goods; ethnic foods; specialty foods; meats and seafood; cooking utensils; condiments; spices; wide selection of Mexican cheeses; prepared take-out foods; and wines. Stores vary in size and character with the neighborhoods they serve. Some have coffee and tea bars, in-store delicatessens and sushi bars. The Fiesta at 1005 Blalock Dr. off I-10 (the Katy Freeway) offers regularly scheduled cooking classes.

The Jamail Family Market, 3333 S. Rice Avenue, south of The Galleria area (621-8030). The last surviving market location for the Jamail family, which brought the concept of gourmet shopping to Houston. This market, opened in May, 1987, is operated by brother and sister, Joe Jamail and Marian Jamail Averyt, and Joe's son, Jim. They specialize in fresh produce, fine meats, seafood and wines. Selections reflect customers favorites. Prepared deli foods include a variety of pasta salads and house specialties including fat-free and low-fat dishes.

Kroger, 3665 Highway 6 at Settler's Way in Sugar Land (980-8888) and 14 Kroger Signature stores (15 by the end of 1996) at various locations throughout the city, are special-concept stores with a wide variety of specialty and gourmet foods and wines. At the Sugar Land store, a wine steward is in charge of what Kroger boasts is the largest selection of wines in a Texas supermarket, and there are more than 400 varieties of produce including a large section of imported and ethnic items and a juice bar.

Signature stores are upscale markets showcasing in-store delicatessens, bakeries and salad bars; specialty foods; fresh meats and seafoods; prepared take-out items; and floral shops. Some do catering.

Randalls Flagship stores (five locations; two more opening in 1996). Top-drawer family-owned and operated supermarkets known for fresh produce; domestic and imported specialty foods; fresh meats and seafood. Flagship stores have in-store bakeries with a pastry chef; delicatessens; coffee-tea bars; fresh salad bars; take-out specialties including an assortment of hand-made pizzas, sandwiches, salads and rotisserie chicken; and floral shops. They offer catering. High-quality packaged meals featuring many good- or better-than-homemade specialties are a holiday tradition.

Randalls celebrates its 30th anniversary in 1996. It has grown from two markets, owned by Houstonians Robert Onstead, Randall C. Barclay and Norm Frewin Sr., to a $2 billion-plus chain with more than 120 stores in Texas including Tom Thumb markets in Dallas. Randalls employs a nutrition specialist who conducts regular supermarket tours.

Rice Epicurean Markets, six locations with more planned. Rice prides itself on stocking the newest and most exclusive specialty foods; produce; meats; emu and other wild game; seafood and fish. Epicurean Markets have in-store delicatessens, coffee and tea bars; wine and cheese collections; wide assortments of pastas, oils, vinegars; hard-to-find spices such as saffron and juniper berries; exotic produce; salad bars; specialty baked goods, desserts and breads. All have extensive prepared food sections and some cook foods to order from in-store "haute grills" with stir-fry stations. Rice is the only supermarket in Houston with in-store shops for Mrs. See's candy and Honey Baked Ham.

Epicurean chefs prepare restaurant-quality take-out foods and packaged dinners for holidays and other special occasions. Catering and in-store floral shops offer complete entertaining services. The Cooking School at the Rice Epicurean Market, 6425 San Felipe, hosts regular classes conducted by director Peg Lee with local and visiting international chefs, cookbook authors and food experts. Call 789-6233.

Whole Foods Markets (three locations) showcase natural foods including organically grown fruits and vegetables; imported and domestic sauces; condiments; a wide variety of bulk grains, cereals, herbs, spices and seasonings; cheeses; dairy products including yogurts and ice creams; frozen foods; additive-free meats and chicken, specialty breads and other baked goods, wines, beers, teas, coffees, health foods, local and regional products including preserves, sauces and cookies.

Stores feature Whole Foods' own brand-name breads; jarred sauces; milk in glass bottles; in-house bakeries, juice bars and delis with an international mix of natural pasta and rice dishes, sandwiches, salads, hot entrees and side dishes. Catering available.

SPECIALTY SHOPS

Ferrari Fresh Pasta, 1715 S. Voss Road (785-6337) and 2033 W. Gray (521-0728) offers an excellent assortment of fresh and custom-made pastas; sauces; condiments; flavored oils and vinegars; baked goods; take-out specialties; decorative serving utensils and accessories as well as full-service catering.

Leibman's Wine & Fine Foods, 14014A Memorial Dr. at Kirkwood (493-3663). Ettienne Leibman hand-picks an extensive collection of wines; hard-to-find spices, oils, vinegars, mustards and other condiments; pesto mixes; imported pastas; candies including Godiva chocolate and sugar-free varieties; specialty bacons and meats such as pancetta and double-smoked bacon; dried mushrooms; olives; chutneys; creme fraiche; and one of the city's best selections of cheeses. In-store deli provides exceptional Chicken Salad Afrique; sandwiches; pasta and rice salads; scones; and incomparable English bread pudding, a house specialty. They specialize in custom gourmet gift baskets.

Richard's Liquors and Fine Wines (several locations). Established in 1949, Richard's has done much to educate Houston's palate for fine wines. Larger stores feature wines from around the world including great vintages and large selections of French Bordeaux and Burgundies; specialty Cognacs, brandies, fruit brandies and Scotches; imported and domestic cheeses; and imported deli meats including Italian pancetta bacon, prosciutto, Westphalian and Black Forest hams. Custom gift baskets are a specialty.

Spec's Liquor Warehouse & a Whole Lot More Store, 2410 Smith Street. Expanded in 1995 to 28,000 square feet, Spec's offers one of the city's most impressive collection of wines, liquors and liqueurs; coffees (more than 90, most roasted in-house) and teas; pates; domestic and imported cheeses (more than 300); spices and seasonings; oils and vinegars; salsas; sauces; pastas (more than 300); preserves; chocolates and other candies; and specialty meats and condiments. In-house delicatessen features made-to-order sandwiches, soups and salads. A LeNotre bakery provides everything from breads to elaborate custom wedding cakes.

Family-owned and operated, Spec's is known for wide selections of wine and specialty foods at good-value prices and for custom-designed gourmet gift baskets.

Yapa Kitchen and Fresh Take Away, 3173 W. Holcombe Blvd. (664-9272). A second shop is opening in the fall of 1996 at Kirby and Westheimer. High-quality prepared foods include fresh pasta; sauces; imported oils; vinegars; cheeses; gourmet foods; Empire and Manna Bakery breads; and desserts from Marilyn Descours' Patisserie Descours. The new store has salad, sandwich and pasta bars. Limited catering available.

MISCELLANEOUS

Cost Plus World Markets entered the Houston retail scene in 1996 with a store at 5125 Richmond Avenue in Richmond Square at Loop 610, and more stores are planned. They offer imported specialty foods — pastas, bread mixes, rice, dried beans, sauces, spices, seasonings, condiments, coffees and teas from all over the world — as well as housewares; linens, pottery, flatware and crystal; decorative objects; furniture; and clothes. Beans can be ground to order for more than 60 coffees and more than 40 teas are stocked.

Williams-Sonoma, 4076 Westheimer (622-4161); 30 Town & Country Village (465-4775); and 1350 Baybrook Mall (480-1705). Williams-Sonoma features everything to outfit the gourmet kitchen from fine-quality cooking utensils and small appliances to table linens and specialty food items. Their forte is gourmet oils and vinegars; pasta; grains; salsas and sauces; china, pottery and table accessories; coffee grinders and coffee makers; spices; cookbooks; gadgets and housewares. Cooking demos and classes offered regularly.

INTERNATIONAL MARKETS

Asian

There are several markets in Chinatown east of Main Street around McKinney and St. Emanuel and another cluster outside Loop 610 on and around Bellaire Boulevard.

Asiatic Import Company, 909 Chartres (227-7979). General Chinese ingredients such as bottled sauces, canned goods, condiments, spices and seasonings as well as cooking utensils.

Daido Market, 11138 Westheimer (785-0815). Japanese market with mostly basic seasonings and sauces, canned goods and limited fresh produce, seafood and tuna.

Diho Market, 9280 Bellaire Blvd. (988-1881). Extensive stock of Chinese and Asian products, fresh meats, fish, wines, sauces, frozen and prepared items, fresh produce and standard sauces and condiments.

Dynasty Supermarket in Dynasty Plaza, 9600 Bellaire Blvd. (995-4088). Full-line supermarket of Asian and Chinese staples, condiments and hot deli items, meats, fresh fish and seafood, wines and beers.

Hong Kong Food Market (three locations). Full-service supermarket with wide range of fresh Asian produce; exotic fruits, juices and vegetables, such as Chinese water spinach; fresh meats, chicken and fish; fresh lobster and other seafoods; sauces; baked goods; tofu; noodles and rice; spices, seasonings and condiments; fresh bamboo leaves.

Kazy's Gourmet, 11346 Westheimer (293-9612), offers Japanese and other Asian ingredients and specialties.

Kim Hung Supermarket, 1005 St. Emanuel (224-6206) and 12320 Bellaire Blvd. (568-3040). Full-service markets specializing in Chinese and Asian imported foods, fresh produce, fresh seafood, sauces, condiments and noodles.

Long Sing Supermarket, 2017 Walker (228-2017). Small scale supermarket with hot deli; fresh produce, meats, fish and seafood; frozen prepared items; condiments, sauces, seasonings, noodles and tofu.

Viet Hoa Supermarket, 8200 Wilcrest at Beechnut (561-8706). Complete supermarket with fish market, produce shop and wide assortment of Asian ingredients including Chinese, Vietnamese and Thai specialties.

Vientiane Market, 6929 Long Point (681-0751). Small but well-stocked market specializing in Thai and Vietnamese foods; some Chinese. Selection of fresh produce; meats and fish; canned goods, traditional sauces, spices, seasonings such as tamarind and yanang leaves, pickles, pickled limes and mixes; cassia flowers, noodles, spring roll skins, coconut milk, palm sugar, curry pastes, fish powder and chilies.

Welcome Food Center, Inc., 9180 Bellaire Blvd. (270-7789). Supermarket featuring fresh meats, fish and seafood, fresh produce, staples of Asian cooking.

Middle Eastern, Persian

Abdallah's, 3939 Hillcroft (952-4747) is a restaurant providing Middle Eastern dishes such as hummus, tabbouleh and vegetables, and stocks a boutique assortment of Middle Eastern spices, herbs, breads, canned goods and prepared desserts. Take-out available.

Antone's Import Co. (several locations). Specializes in spices, sauces, Middle Eastern and other imported foods and wines along with world-class poor boys.

Droubi's Imports (four locations and three more planned in 1996). Restaurants at several locations including Droubi's Bakery & Delicatessen, 7333 Hillcroft (988-5891); and 7807 Kirby Drive (790-0101). Feature Middle Eastern and European imports and other specialty foods from around the world. Known for Middle Eastern breads, hummus, falafel, tabbouleh, shish kabab and deli classics. Take-out and full catering available.

Phoenicia Specialty Foods, 12126 Westheimer (558-0416). Middle Eastern and Mediterranean grains, rice, beans, sauces, spices, pastries, meats, cheeses and other gourmet foods at top-value prices. Many available in bulk. Phoenicia Deli, which offers some products and take-out Middle Eastern specialties, such as tabbouleh and falafel, is nearby.

Super Sahel, 5627 Hillcroft (266-7360). Small shop with necessities for Persian cooking such as basmati rice, couscous, pickled garlic, ghormeh sabji herb mix, barberries, canned okra, sumac and other traditional spices, sesame candy; pomegranate and other exotic syrups and preserves, chutneys.

Super Vanak International Food Market & Deli, 5692 Hillcroft (952-7676). Stocks all the staples of Persian and other Middle Eastern cuisines — sour cherry and pineapple syrups, mint water, barberries; fig jam; cherry, pergamot, carrot and quince preserves; teas and coffee; pickles; sumac and spice mixes; pickled lemons; camomile flowers; curry pastes; chutneys; fesenjoon (a mixture of walnuts, tomato paste, mushrooms, pomegranate paste and juice, onion and canola oil); taftoon bread; basmati rice; tahini; dried fruits.

Indian

India Grocers, 6606 Southwest Freeway at Hillcroft (266-7717) and 5604 Hillcroft (782-8500) are stocked with classic spices and foods from India, Pakistan and around the world. Wide variety of rices; dal (lentils); spices; gram flour (besan); pickles; chutneys and other condiments; ghee (clarified, reduced butter); pistachios, peanuts, cashews, almonds and other nuts; tahini and other pastes; mixes; fresh produce including popular Indian vegetables and mangos; breads; desserts; frozen and canned foods at good-value prices.

Patel Brothers, 5815 Hillcroft (784-8332). Stocks all the accoutrements of Indian cooking from almond oil and fresh curry leaves to exotic ice creams. Good source for saffron and other spices; raisins and figs; cashews, pistachios and other nuts; ginger and garlic pastes; dal (lentils); a wide variety of chutneys; tamarind; and fresh fruit, especially mangos in season.

RECIPE NUTRITIONAL ANALYSIS

The nutrient information below was calculated by computer nutrient analysis of each recipe and the recipe prepared according to the modification tip. Every effort has been made to check the accuracy of these numbers. However, because numerous variables account for a wide range of nutrients in foods, all analyses that appear should be considered approximate.

The nutrient analysis is for one serving, unless a different number of servings is suggested in the modification tip. If you serve more or less than the suggested serving, you must adjust the nutrient numbers. If a range of servings is given, the first number is used for analysis.

The nutrient analysis of each recipe includes all the ingredients that are listed in that recipe, except for ingredients for which no amount is given, for instance "salt to taste," or ingredients labeled as optional. If an ingredient is presented with an option ("1 cup chicken or vegetable broth" or "2 to 4 tablespoons of butter"), the first item or number listed was used to calculate the nutrition information.

* *Recipes modified according to instructions at the end of the regular recipe designated with an apple. Regular recipes with an asterisk meet guidelines for a healthy recipe.*

	Portion	Calories	Protein (g)	Carbohydrate (g)	Fat (g)	% Fat Calories	Cholesterol (mg)	Sodium (mg)	Dietary Fiber (g)
Acorn Squash Soup (Rivoli)	1 serving	196	4	22	12	51	41	308	3
*Modified Recipe	1 serving	158	7	26	4	23	13	56	3
Adam's Mark Bread Pudding/Sauce (Deco)	1 serving	1000	18	119	51	46	411	509	0
Amaretto Cheesecake (Redwood)	1 serving	1014	9	123	55	48	196	489	1
Ancho Chili Soup (Post Oak)	1 serving	114	11	6	4	31	32	1123	1
*Modified Recipe	1 serving	55	5	5	1	18	29	90	1
Anthony's Seared Shrimp/Mango Salsa	1 serving	333	21	31	15	40	174	207	4
*Modified Recipe	1 serving	243	21	31	5	18	174	207	4
Balsamic Angel Hair Pasta/Chicken(Post Oak)	1 serving	1290	107	80	58	41	409	727	5
*Modified Recipe	1 serving	696	53	80	17	23	191	553	5
Black Bean Burrito (VIVA)	1 burrito	318	12	44	12	33	0	604	6
*Modified Recipe	1 burrito	291	12	44	9	28	0	604	6
Blackberry Crustade (Anthony's)	1 serving	1193	9	138	70	52	186	706	6
Blanc Mange Romanoff (Rivoli)	1 serving	424	6	48	21	44	78	70	1
Boneless Quail & Vegetable Flambe (Empress)	1 serving	384	24	14	24	56	10	1635	0
*Modified Recipe	1 serving	258	22	14	11	39	9	1430	0
Caponata (Riviera)	1 serving	408	2	12	41	87	0	2137	1
*Modified Recipe	1 serving	111	2	12	7	54	0	538	1
Caramanolas (Churrascos)	1 serving	508	28	26	71	75	18	117	1
Carpaccio of Beefsteak Tomatoes (DeVille)	1 serving	214	2	7	21	83	0	51	2
*Modified Recipe	1 serving	55	2	7	3	38	0	51	2
Cerdo a la Puchica (Churrascos)	1 serving	638	44	28	39	54	171	405	2
*Modified Recipe	1 serving	432	43	28	16	34	146	247	2

	Portion	Calories	Protein (g)	Carbohydrate (g)	Fat (g)	% Fat Calories	Cholesterol (mg)	Sodium (mg)	Dietary Fiber (g)
Chicken Kabab (Cafe Caspian)	1 serving	962	78	24	65	58	173	2449	3
*Modified Recipe	1 serving	688	78	24	34	44	142	200	3
Chicken Positano (Grotto)	1 serving	1180	76	92	54	41	347	2767	8
*Modified Recipe	1 serving	888	55	90	32	32	197	2000	8
Chilled Leek Soup (Chez Nous)	1 serving	342	4	6	34	89	113	529	0
*Modified Recipe	1 serving	109	5	10	6	45	16	126	0
Chocolate Brownie Fudge (Empress)	1 bar	213	2	21	15	60	70	10	1
Chocolate Peanut Butter Fudge Pie (Brennan's)	1 serving	1060	22	74	83	66	193	589	4
Cornflake Cinnamon Raisin Toast (Deco)	1 serving	405	8	26	31	67	227	370	0
*Modified Recipe	1 serving	173	8	26	4	19	74	274	0
Crispy Chicken with Lemon Sauce (Empress)	1 serving	329	14	32	16	44	88	299	0
Fedilini Buongustaio (Damian's)	1 serving	959	62	65	50	47	356	1775	1
*Modified Recipe	1 serving	279	24	26	8	27	101	601	1
*Figs & Berries with Sabayon & Sorbet (Chez Nous)	1 serving	414	5	74	12	25	182	50	11
Frijoles a la Charras Poblanos (Rancho Tejas)	1 serving	341	22	42	10	25	13	1736	6
*Modified Recipe	1 serving	292	16	41	8	24	12	232	6
Gazpacho El Rey (LaTour d'Argent)	1 serving	109	2	13	6	47	0	17	3
*Modified Recipe	1 serving	79	2	13	3	29	0	17	3
Grand Marnier Souffle (LaTour d'Argent)	1 serving	953	24	163	18	17	459	301	0
Grilled Beef Tenderloin (DeVille)	1 serving	1170	69	111	54	40	164	318	9
*Modified Recipe	1 serving	986	69	111	33	29	119	320	9
*Grilled Caribbean Shrimp (Brownstone)	1 serving	415	20	45	15	33	135	545	1
Grilled Corn Soup with Pico de Gallo (Houstonian)	1 serving	273	12	34	12	37	3	1446	5
*Modified Recipe	1 serving	182	10	28	4	21	3	1036	5
Grilled Pork Chops & Fruit Chutney (Riviera)	10 ounces	537	45	36	24	40	148	119	4
*Modified Recipe	6 ounces	379	27	36	15	34	89	73	4
Grilled Shrimp with Risotto (Riviera)	1 serving	848	32	67	50	53	170	2073	1
*Modified Recipe	1 serving	500	20	65	17	31	113	868	1
Grilled Stuffed Flounder (Rancho Tejas)	1 serving	1592	79	79	106	60	421	3550	1
*Modified Recipe	1 serving	593	58	35	24	37	238	1041	1
Grilled Quail & Mushroom Salad (Brownstone)	1 serving	997	23	13	93	82	21	464	2
*Modified Recipe	1 serving	405	23	10	30	65	10	252	2
Insalata del Cuoco (Cavatore)	1 serving	291	24	16	17	48	174	329	6
*Modified Recipe	1 serving	202	24	16	6	27	174	329	6
Joey's Nutty Salad (La Griglia)	1 serving	946	13	44	84	77	30	394	5
*Modified Recipe	1 serving	272	7	34	14	43	30	179	4
Lamb Chops Arno (Damian's)	1 serving	402	32	1	27	59	120	230	0
*Modified Recipe	1 serving	321	32	1	18	52	105	153	0
Lemon Chess Pie (Moose Cafe)	1 serving	432	5	61	20	41	164	393	0
Mama's Carrot Cake (Third Coast)	1 serving	1241	12	129	78	55	186	331	3
*Mango Rice Pudding (Houstonian)	1 serving	270	7	54	3	9	11	285	1

	Portion	Calories	Protein (g)	Carbohydrate (g)	Fat (g)	% Fat Calories	Cholesterol (mg)	Sodium (mg)	Dietary Fiber (g)
Marinara Sauce (Cavatore)	1 serving	357	5	26	28	67	0	46	6
*Modified Recipe	1 serving	178	5	26	8	38	0	46	6
Medallions of Venison (Rotisserie)	1 serving	981	48	17	79	72	288	1395	1
*Modified Recipe	1 serving	493	46	17	24	45	197	678	1
Nantucket Bleu Spinach Salad (Redwood)	1 serving	525	8	23	47	77	11	656	5
*Modified Recipe	1 serving	241	6	23	16	56	6	552	5
Osso Buco with Risotto alla Milanese (Tony's)	1 serving	642	34	36	39	54	98	1125	6
*Modified Recipe	1 serving	410	32	36	14	30	105	767	6
Pan-Seared Pork Tenderloin with Chutney(Deco)	1/8 recipe	1475	84	116	78	47	259	1184	8
*Modified Recipe	1/12 recipe	788	48	73	35	39	165	487	4
Pargo Americas (Americas)	1 serving	530	50	24	26	44	153	249	2
*Modified Recipe	1 serving	441	50	24	14	29	128	256	2
*Peach Melba Smoothie (VIVA)	1 serving	208	2	49	0	2	0	2	4
Peanuts & Ginger Soup (Empress)	1 serving	653	20	58	42	54	0	708	5
Pecan Cobbler (Rancho Tejas)	1 serving	737	7	93	38	46	181	609	1
Penne Pasta with Arugula (Grotto)	1 serving	756	30	96	31	36	108	429	9
*Modified Recipe	1 serving	666	30	96	21	27	108	429	9
Penne Pasta with Chicken & Spinach Sauce(DeVille)	1 serving	781	35	64	44	50	197	539	5
*Modified Recipe	1 serving	538	32	63	18	30	120	353	5
Pepper Crusted Sea Bass (Riviera)	1 serving	484	37	34	23	42	71	746	4
*Modified Recipe	1 serving	415	37	34	15	32	71	707	4
Pollo Menichino (Damian's)	1 serving	656	42	9	48	66	177	994	2
*Modified Recipe	1 serving	354	37	9	16	41	93	455	2
Praline Ice Cream Parfait (Rotisserie)	1 serving	1561	10	124	113	62	516	203	2
Pumpkin Cream Brule (DeVille)	1 serving	803	13	76	52	57	483	280	1
Ranchero Sauce (VIVA)	1 serving	92	1	7	7	67	0	270	1
*Modified Recipe	1 serving	32	1	7	0	9	0	137	1
Rice with Lima Beans (Cafe Caspian)	1/6 recipe	680	13	101	24	32	62	2417	4
*Modified Recipe	1/9 recipe	408	9	67	11	24	28	612	3
Rigatoni alla Verdure (Cavatore)	1 serving	859	49	88	35	36	318	373	6
*Modified Recipe	1 serving	760	48	86	24	29	306	360	6
Risotto alla Milanese (Tony's)	1 serving	464	14	61	15	29	18	1380	1
*Modified Recipe	1 serving	432	9	60	14	29	17	734	1
Roasted Peppers with Fontina (Tony's)	1 serving	149	7	1	13	77	62	195	0
Roast Lamb Rack (LaTour d'Argent)	1 serving	529	47	11	32	55	164	494	0
*Modified Recipe	1 serving	478	47	11	26	50	148	493	0
Salmon Cakes (Moose Cafe)	1 serving	210	8	15	13	56	40	515	1
*Modified Recipe	1 serving	109	8	15	2	14	9	131	1
Saute of Chanterelle Mushrooms (Chez Nous)	1 serving	312	8	17	25	69	61	279	2
*Modified Recipe	1 serving	138	7	20	4	27	7	161	2

	Portion	Calories	Protein (g)	Carbohydrate (g)	Fat (g)	% Fat Calories	Cholesterol (mg)	Sodium (mg)	Dietary Fiber (g)
Scallopini di Pollo (Cavatore)	1 serving	1215	86	27	84	62	311	2076	5
*Modified Recipe	1 serving	522	60	26	18	32	177	478	5
Shrimp Damian (Damian's)	1 serving	687	34	0	59	77	460	1033	0
*Modified Recipe	1 serving	235	34	0	8	31	321	603	0
Smoked Chicken Salad (Rotisserie)	1 serving	762	51	54	40	46	322	821	7
*Modified Recipe	1 serving	402	34	51	8	17	180	1001	7
Smoked Salmon Julienne (LaTour d'Argent)	1 serving	93	8	2	5	53	10	402	1
*Modified Recipe	1 serving	61	8	2	2	29	10	449	1
Smoked Tomato & Spinach Dip (Moose Cafe)	1/2 cup	293	7	6	27	81	88	367	1
*Modified Recipe	1/2 cup	112	11	12	3	20	9	447	1
Snapper La Griglia (La Griglia)	1 serving	807	56	36	47	53	200	509	0
*Modified Recipe	1 serving	637	56	36	27	40	165	392	0
*Spinach Enchiladas (VIVA)	1 serving	319	23	36	13	37	41	763	4
Spinach Quesadillas (Moose Cafe)	1 serving	390	12	41	20	46	17	558	0
*Modified Recipe	1 serving	293	13	41	8	26	14	516	0
Steamed Striped Bass with Spinach (Chez Nous)	1 serving	487	41	7	33	61	160	522	3
*Modified Recipe	1 serving	360	41	7	19	47	121	376	3
Stuffed Dover Sole (Rivoli)	1 serving	660	73	9	37	50	287	1082	1
*Modified Recipe	1 serving	489	74	10	15	29	219	1055	1
Stuffed Jalapenos (Rancho Tejas)	1 serving	445	16	28	30	61	167	2346	4
*Modified Recipe	1 serving	323	16	28	16	45	74	1574	4
Sweet Potato-Chipotle Bisque (Brownstone)	1 serving	329	8	17	25	67	86	827	2
*Modified Recipe	1 serving	135	6	22	2	11	6	103	2
Texas Creole Barbecue Shrimp (Brennan's)	1 serving	1857	57	211	92	44	601	4740	4
*Modified Recipe	1 serving	286	25	29	8	26	194	891	3
Third Coast's Crabcakes Entree (Third Coast)	1 serving	1182	40	24	105	78	450	2396	4
*Modified Recipe	1 serving	362	38	22	13	33	201	1850	2
Torta de Queso y Maiz (Americas)	1 serving	450	8	31	34	66	158	364	0
*Modified Recipe	1 serving	326	9	33	19	50	107	508	0
Tournedos Voronoff (Rivoli)	1 serving	541	34	6	40	66	177	135	0
*Modified Recipe	1 serving	326	38	11	11	31	98	187	0
VIVA! Black Beans (VIVA)	1 serving	355	19	54	8	20	0	269	9
*Modified Recipe	1 serving	296	19	54	1	4	0	269	9
VIVA! Pasta (VIVA)	1 serving	873	32	100	40	40	10	514	9
*Modified Recipe	1 serving	675	32	100	18	23	10	514	9
Warm Bittersweet Chocolate Torte (Riviera)	1 serving	792	12	86	51	54	357	53	0
Yakitori Salmon Salad (Houstonian)	1 serving	512	29	70	10	17	82	2445	2
*Modified Recipe	1 serving	511	29	70	10	17	82	1320	2
Yogurt & Spinach Dip (Cafe Caspian)	1 serving	134	5	8	10	62	11	351	1
*Modified Recipe	1 serving	99	7	11	4	32	2	376	1

INDEX

AMERICAS 15
ANTHONY'S 19
Appetizers
Caponata (Riviera Grill) 88
Caramanolas (Churrascos) 17
Roasted Peppers with Fontina
 (Tony's) 100
Salmon Cakes (Moose Cafe) 73
Smoked Salmon Julienne with Endive
 (La Tour d'Argent) 68
Smoked Tomato and Spinach Dip
 (Moose Cafe) 72
Spinach Quesadillas
 (Moose Cafe) 72
Stuffed Jalapenos (Rancho Tejas) 82
Yogurt and Spinach Dip
 (Cafe Caspian) 34

Bailey, Melissa (Redwood Grill) 77
Bass, Doug (The Brownstone) 27
Bastankhan, Massoud "Max"
 (Cafe Caspian) 33
Brennan-Martin, Alex (Brennan's, Third
 Coast) 23
BRENNAN'S 23
BROWNSTONE, THE 27
Butera, Joseph A. "Bubba"
 (Damian's) 45

CAFE CASPIAN 33
Cantu, Rosi (Rivoli) 89
CAVATORE 37
Cavatore, Giancarlo (Cavatore) 37
Chen, Scott (Empress) 39
CHEZ NOUS 41
CHURRASCOS 15
Cordua, Glenn (Americas,
 Churrascos) 15
Cordua, Michael (Americas,
 Churrascos) 15
Cox, Mark (Tony's) 99

DAMIAN'S 45
DECO, Adam's Mark Hotel 49
Drought, Shelly (Redwood Grill) 77

Desserts
Amaretto Cheesecake/Amaretto
 Glaze/Chocolate Sauce
 (Redwood Grill) 80
Blackberry Crustade (Anthony's) 20
BlancMange Romanoff (Rivoli) 92
Bread Pudding/Kentucky Bourbon Sauce
 (Deco, Adam's Mark) 52
Chocolate Brownie Fudge
 (Empress) 62
Chocolate Peanut Butter Fudge Pie
 (Brennan's) 25
Figs and Berries/Sabayon/Key Lime
 Sorbet (Chez Nous) 44
Grand Marnier Souffle (La Tour
 d'Argent) 70
Key Lime Sorbet/Figs and Berries,
 Sabayon with (Chez Nous)...............44
Lemon Chess Pie (Moose Cafe) 74
Mama's Carrot Cake (Brennan's,
 Third Coast) 25
Mango Rice Pudding/Ginger Candy
 Crust (The Houstonian) 66
Pecan Cobbler (Rancho Tejas) 84
Praline Ice Cream Parfait/ Caramelized
 Pecans/Chocolate Sauce
 (Rotisserie) 96
Pumpkin Cream Brule with Fresh Berry
 Compote (DeVille) 58
Torta de Queso y Maiz – Cheesecake
 with Sweet Corn (Americas) 16
Warm Bittersweet Chocolate Torte
 (Riviera Grill) 88
DeVILLE, Four Seasons Hotel 55

EMPRESS 59

Ferre, Luigi (Damian's) 45
Fish and Seafood
Crab
 Crabmeat Shrimp Stuffing, Grilled
  Stuffed Flounder with
  (Rancho Tejas) 83
 Stuffed Dover Sole (Rivoli) 91
 Third Coast Crabcakes/Lemon Butter
  Sauce/ Pico de Gallo
  (Third Coast) 26

Grilled Stuffed Flounder/Crabmeat
 Shrimp Stuffing with
 (Rancho Tejas) 83
Pepper-Crusted Sea Bass, Kalamata
 Olives, Garlic, Capers, Tomato
 Ragout (Riviera Grill) 86
Steamed Striped Bass/Wilted
 Spinach/Sweet Pepper and Lime
 Sauce (Chez Nous) 43
Stuffed Dover Sole (Rivoli) 91
Salmon
Salmon Cakes (Moose Cafe) 73
Smoked Salmon Julienne with Endive
 (La Tour d'Argent) 68
Yakitori Salmon Salad/Buckwheat
 Noodles/Ponzu Dressing
 (The Houstonian) 65
Shrimp
Anthony's Seared Shrimp with Spicy
 Mango Salsa 20
Grilled Caribbean Shrimp/Cuban BBQ
 Sauce/Orange-Jalapeno Risotto
 (The Brownstone) 28
Grilled Shrimp with Roasted Red
 Pepper Risotto (Riviera Grill) 86
Shrimp Damian (Damian's) 46
Shrimp/Crabmeat Stuffing,
 Grilled Stuffed Flounder with
 (Rancho Tejas) 83
Texas Creole Barbecued Shrimp/Jicama
 Salad/Texas Cornbread Pudding
 (Brennan's) 24
Snapper
Pargo Americas (Americas) 16
Snapper La Griglia (La Griglia) 21
Fisher, Ethel (Post Oak Grill, Redwood
 Grill) 77
Fruit
Figs and Berries/Sabayon/Key Lime
 Sorbet (Chez Nous) 44
Fresh Berry Compote, Pumpkin Cream
 Brule with (DeVille) 58
Granny Smith Vinaigrette, Pan-Seared
 Pork Tenderloin/Macadamia Nut
 Chutney with
 (Deco, Adam's Mark) 51

Papaya Salsa, Smoked Chicken Salad with (Rotisserie for Beef and Bird) 94
Scotch Bonnet Fruit Chutney, Grilled Center-Cut Pork Chops with (Riviera Grill) 87

Gibson, Florence C. (Brennan's) 23
GROTTO 99
Gutknecht, Pierre (Rivoli) 89

HOUSTONIAN, THE 63

Jachmich, Manfred (Post Oak Grill, Redwood Grill) 77

Knott, Russell (Third Coast) 23

Lahham, Sonny (Cavatore, La Tour d'Argent) 67
LA GRIGLIA 19
LA TOUR d'ARGENT 67
Liebrum, Roger (Viva!) 103

Maldonado, Edi (Viva!) 103
Malla, Hessni (La Tour d'Argent) 67
Mallett, Alan (Moose Cafe) 71
Mandola, Frank B. (Damian's) 45
Mannke, Joe (Rotisserie for Beef and Bird) 93
McCarley, Pat (Rancho Tejas) 81
McMillian, Bruce (Anthony's) 19
Mills, Jim (The Houstonian) 63

Meat
Beef
Grilled Beef Tenderloin on Potato-Thyme Cake, Chipotle Cream (DeVille, Four Seasons Hotel) 57
Tournedos Voronoff (Rivoli) 92
Lamb
Lamb Chops Arno (Damian's) 46
Roast Lamb Rack with Herb and Mustard (La Tour d'Argent) 69
Osso Buco with Balsamic Vinegar/Risotto alla Milanese (Tony's) 100
Pork
Cerdo a la Puchica (Churrascos) 18

Grilled Center-Cut Pork Chops/Scotch Bonnet Fruit Chutney (Riviera Grill) 87
Pan-Seared Pork Tenderloin/Macadamia Nut Chutney/Granny Smith Vinaigrette (Deco, Adam's Mark Hotel) 50
Venison, Medallions of with Chile Pepper Sauce (Rotisserie for Beef and Bird) 95
Miscellaneous
Black Bean Burrito (Viva!) 104
Caramelized Onions, Joey's Nutty Salad with (La Griglia) 22
Caramelized Pecans, Praline Ice Cream Parfait with (Rotisserie for Beef and Bird) 96
Chicken Marinade, Pollo Menichino with (Damian's) 47
Cornflake Cinnamon Raisin Toast (Deco, Adam's Mark Hotel) 51
Peach Melba Smoothie (Viva!) 106
Texas Cornbread Pudding, Texas Creole Barbecue Shrimp with Jicama Salad (Brennan's) 24
MOOSE CAFE 71

Pasta, Rice
Pasta
Balsamic Angel Hair Pasta with Chicken (Post Oak Grill) 79
Buckwheat Noodles/Yakitori Salmon Salad/Ponzu Dressing (The Houstonian) 65
Fedilini Buongustaio (Damian's) 48
Penne Pasta with Arugula (Grotto) 101
Penne Pasta with Sauteed Chicken and Spinach Cream Sauce (DeVille, Four Seasons Hotel) 56
Rigatoni alla Verdure (Cavatore).......39
Viva! Pasta (Viva!) 105
Rice
Mango Rice Pudding with Ginger Candy Crust (The Houstonian) 66

Orange-Jalapeno Risotto, Grilled Caribbean Shrimp with Cuban Barbecue Sauce and (The Brownstone) 29
Rice with Lima Beans (Cafe Caspian) 36
Risotto alla Milanese, Osso Buco with Balsamic Vinegar (Tony's) 101
Roasted Red Pepper Risotto with Grilled Shrimp (Riviera Grill) 86

POST OAK GRILL 77
Poultry
Chicken, Balsamic Angel Hair Pasta with (Post Oak Grill) 79
Chicken Kabab (Cafe Caspian) 35
Chicken Positano with Italian Spinach (Grotto) 102
Chicken Sauteed, Penne Pasta, Spinach Cream Sauce with (DeVille, Four Seasons Hotel) 56
Crispy Chicken with Lemon Sauce (Empress) 61
Pollo Menichino (Damian's)...............47
Scallopini di Pollo (Cavatore) 40
Quail
Boneless Quail with Shredded Vegetables Flambe (Empress) 60
Grilled Quail and Portobello Mushroom Salad (The Brownstone) 30

RANCHO TEJAS 81
REDWOOD GRILL 77
RIVIERA GRILL 85
RIVOLI 89
ROTISSERIE FOR BEEF AND BIRD 93
Ruppe, Tony (DeVille, Four Seasons Hotel) 55

Sadler, Bill (Moose Cafe) 71
Sheely, John (Riviera Grill) 85
Salads
Carpaccio of Beefsteak Tomatoes with Spinach, Arugula and Balsamic Vinaigrette (DeVille, Four Seasons Hotel) 58

Granny Smith Vinaigrette, Pan Seared
Pork Tenderloin/Macadamia Chutney
with (Deco, Adam's Mark)...................51
Grilled Quail and Portobello Mushroom
Salad
(The Brownstone) 30
Insalata del Cuoco (Cavatore) 38
Jicama Salad, Texas Creole Barbecue
Shrimp and Texas Cornbread Pudding
with (Brennan's) 24
Joey's Nutty Salad/Honey Balsamic
Dressing/Caramelized Onions
(La Griglia) 22
Nantucket Bleu Spinach Salad
(Redwood Grill) 79
Smoked Chicken Salad with Papaya
Salsa (Rotisserie for Beef
and Bird) 94
Yakatori Salmon Salad/Buckwheat
Noodles/Ponzu Dressing
(The Houstonian) 65

Salsas
Avocado Pico de Gallo, Grilled Corn
Soup with (The Houstonian) 64
Papaya Salsa, Smoked Chicken Salad with
(Rotisserie for Beef and Bird) 94
Pico de Gallo, Crabcakes, Lemon Butter
Sauce and (Third Coast) 26
Spicy Mango Salsa, Seared Shrimp with
(Anthony's) 20

Sauces
Amaretto Glaze, Chocolate Sauce,
Amaretto Cheesecake with (Redwood
Grill) 80
Barbecue Sauce Base, Texas Creole
Barbecue Shrimp/Jicama Salad/Texas
Cornbread Pudding (Brennan's) 24
Champagne Sauce, Snapper La Griglia
with (La Griglia) 21
Chile-Pepper Sauce, Venison Medallions
with (Rotisserie for Beef and Bird) 95
Chipotle Cream, Grilled Beef Tenderloin
on Potato-Thyme Cakes with (DeVille,
Four Seasons Hotel) 57
Chocolate Sauce, Praline Ice Cream
Parfait, with (Rotisserie for Beef
and Bird) 96

Cream Sauce Base, Pomodoro Sauce,
Fedilini Buongustaio with (Damian's)...48
Cuban BBQ Sauce, Grilled Caribbean
Shrimp, Orange-Jalapeno Risotto with
(The Brownstone) 29
Kentucky Bourbon Sauce, Bread Pudding
with (Deco, Adam's
Mark Hotel) 52
Lemon Butter Sauce, Cerdo a la Puchica
with (Churrascos) 18
Lemon Butter Sauce, Crabcakes, Pico de
Gallo with (Third Coast) 26
Lemon Sauce, Crispy Chicken with
(Empress) 61
Marinara Sauce (Cavatore) 38
Marsala Wine Sauce, Chicken Positano
(Grotto) 102
Ranchero Sauce (Viva!) 105
Red Pepper Sauce, Caramanolas with
(Churrascos) 17
Romanoff Sauce, Blanc Mange with
(Rivoli) 92
Spinach Cream Sauce, Penne Pasta,
Sauteed Chicken with (DeVille, Four
Seasons Hotel) 56
Sabayon, Figs and Berries/Key Lime
Sorbet with (Chez Nous) 44
Sweet Pepper and Lime Sauce, Steamed
Striped Bass with
(Chez Nous) 43
Tejas Pecan Butter, Grilled Stuffed
Flounder, Crabmeat Shrimp Stuffing
with (Rancho Tejas) 83
Soto, Rosalinda (Rivoli) 89

Soup
Acorn Squash Soup (Rivoli) 90
Ancho Chili Soup (Post Oak Grill) 78
Chilled Leek Soup (Chez Nous) 42
Gazpacho El Rey (La Tour d'Argent) 68
Grilled Corn Soup with Avocado Pico de
Gallo (The Houstonian) 64
Peanuts and Ginger Soup
(Empress) 61
Sweet Potato-Chipotle Bisque
(The Brownstone) 25
Theriot, Beau (The Brownstone) 27
THIRD COAST 23

TONY'S 99
Torres, Greg (Cavatore) 19

Vallone, Tony 99
Vegetables
Acorn Squash Soup (Rivoli) 90
Black Beans (Viva!) 104
Caponata (Riviera Grill) 88
Chilled Leek Soup (Chez Nous) 42
Frijoles a las Charras Poblanos
(Rancho Tejas) 84
Gazpacho El Rey
(La Tour d'Argent) 68
Grilled Corn Soup with Avocado Pico de
Gallo (The Houstonian) 64
Lima Beans, Rice with
(Cafe Caspian) 36
Mushrooms
Portobello Mushroom Salad, Grilled
Quail and (The Brownstone) 30
Sauté of Chanterelle Mushrooms with
Corn (Chez Nous) 42
Potato-Thyme Cake, Grilled Beef
Tenderloin, Chipotle Cream, with
(DeVille, Four Seasons Hotel) 57
Spinach
Italian Spinach, Chicken Positano
with (Grotto) 102
Spinach Enchiladas (Viva!) 106
Spinach Quesadillas
(Moose Cafe) 72
Wilted Spinach, Steamed Striped Bass,
Sweet Pepper and Lime Sauce with
(Chez Nous) 43
Yogurt and Spinach Dip
(Cafe Caspian) 34
Shredded Vegetables Flambe, Boneless
Quail with (Empress) 60
Texas Cornbread Pudding, Texas Creole
Barbecued Shrimp, Jicama Salad with
(Brennan's) 24
VIVA! 103

Walker, Carl (Brennan's) 23

FRAN FAUNTLEROY

Fran Fauntleroy was inspired to begin her own company, Houston Gourmet Publishing, after writing and marketing two successful cookbooks, "Six Flew Over The Cuckoo's Kitchens" and "Cuckoo, Too," with six lifelong friends.

She has been responsible for six Houston restaurant cookbooks and eight Houston menu guides, the latest of which is Houston Gourmet Today. She has published and sold more than 165,000 of these books in the past 18 years!

Her high energy and great interest in Houston's fine restaurants is the springboard that keeps her busy thinking of new ways to spotlight the ever-changing dining scene.

Following the success of Dallas Is Cooking!, a cookbook highlighting the restaurants for which that city has become famous, Fran then initiated Houston Is Cooking! with Ann Criswell. They have now joined together to create Houston Is Cooking The Best. This special gourmet collector's cookbook showcases the city's top restaurants and chefs who have successfully brought Houston recognition on a national level.

In addition to being a wife to John, mother of three grown children — Glenda, Shelley and Parker — their special spouses Robby and Mitchell — and grandmother to Ginny, Rob and Parker, the joys of her life, she continues to be active within the community.

ANN STEINER

Ann Steiner is a syndicated microwave columnist who with her co-author, CiCi Williamson, created and published two microwave cookbooks — "Microwave Know-How" and "Micro Quick!" The duo also developed and appeared in a microwave cooking video and have written articles for several professional and popular publications.

Ann's varied interests in the culinary arena include: cookbook editing (this is her second "Houston Is Cooking" publication), recipe development and testing for major food companies, cooking seminars and teacher training. In addition, Ann also served as a judge for the national Beef Cook-Off and Celebrity Microwave Cooking Contest.

She received a Master's Degree from Ohio State University and a Bachelor's Degree from Miami University (Ohio). In 1992, the Federation of Houston Professional Women selected Ann as one of their "Woman of Excellence" honorees. She is a member of the Houston Culinary Guild, Les Dames d'Escoffier and the International Association of Culinary Professionals.

Married to high-school classmate Bill, Ann is also mother of Cindy, Cathy and Jeff, mother-in-law of Steve Walker and Mike Knight and Nanna to Christa and Madelyn.

WHO'S WHO

Key to Back Cover Photograph

1 **Ann Criswell,** *Author*
2 **Linda McDonald,** *Nutritionist*
3 **Fran Fauntleroy,** *Publisher*
4 **Jim Mills,** *The Houstonian*
5 **Joe Mannke,** *Rotisserie for Beef and Bird*
6 **Mark Cox,** *Tony's*
7 **Pat McCarley,** *Rancho Tejas*
8 **Russell Knott,** *Third Coast*
9 **Tony Ruppe,** *DeVille, Four Seasons*

10 **J.M. Matos,** *Deco at the Adams Mark*
11 **Ben Bailey**
12 **Melissa Bailey,** *Redwood Grill*
13 **Carl Walker,** *Brennan's*
14 **Luigi Ferre,** *Damian's*
15 **Douglas Bass,** *The Brownstone*
16 **Shelley Cox,** *Project Assistant*
17 **Polo Becerra,** *Post Oak Grill*
18 **Scott Chen,** *Empress*

19 **Denman Moody,** *Wines*
20 **Pierre Gutknecht,** *Rivoli*
21 **John Sheely,** *Riviera Grill*
22 **Refugia Martinez,** *La Tour d'Argent*
23 **Carlos O. Castellanos,** *Churrascos*
24 **Gregory Torres,** *Cavatore*
25 **Alan Mallett,** *Moose Cafe*
26 **Humberto Molina-Segura,** *Americas*

ORDER FORM

Name _____

Address _____

City _____ State _____ Zip _____

Telephone _____

Houston Is Cooking The Best

$19.95 per copy plus $2.00 handling and postage per book.

Make checks or money orders payable to Houston Gourmet *and mail to:*

Houston Gourmet
2 Pine Forest
Houston, Texas 77056

Texas residents, also add applicable state sales tax

OTHER BOOKS AVAILABLE
Houston Gourmet Today

Menus, LiteFare, To Go and Who's Where
A menu guide to fine dining with Healthy Eating Guidelines, and To Go information.

$15.95 per copy plus $2.00 handling and postage per book.

QUANTITY	PRICE	SHIPPING	TAX	SUBTOTAL

TOTAL THIS ORDER _____

Wholesale orders are welcome!
Buyers please contact Fran Fauntleroy at
713-621-3230 *to place an order.*

ORDER FORM

Name _____

Address _____

City _____ State _____ Zip _____

Telephone _____

Houston Is Cooking The Best

$19.95 per copy plus $2.00 handling and postage per book.

Make checks or money orders payable to Houston Gourmet *and mail to:*

Houston Gourmet
2 Pine Forest
Houston, Texas 77056

Texas residents, also add applicable state sales tax

OTHER BOOKS AVAILABLE
Houston Gourmet Today

Menus, LiteFare, To Go and Who's Where
A menu guide to fine dining with Healthy Eating Guidelines, and To Go information.

$15.95 per copy plus $2.00 handling and postage per book.

QUANTITY	PRICE	SHIPPING	TAX	SUBTOTAL

TOTAL THIS ORDER _____

Wholesale orders are welcome!
Buyers please contact Fran Fauntleroy at
713-621-3230 *to place an order.*